HOME BAKED BREAD AND CAKES

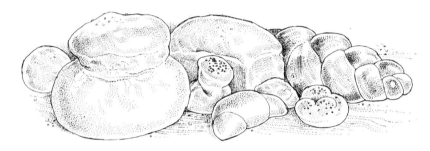

Mary Norwak

HAMLYN
London · New York · Sydney · Toronto

Acknowledgements

The author and publishers thank the following
for their co-operation in supplying photographs
for this book:

**Trex Cookery Service (J. Bibby Foods Products
Limited):** page 23

Kake Brand: page 27

Gale's Honey: page 31

Libby McNeill and Libby Limited: page 59

First published in 1966 by
Countrywise Books, Agricultural Press Limited
This edition published in 1973 by
The Hamlyn Publishing Group Limited
Astronaut House, Feltham, Middlesex, England
Fourth impression 1977

© Copyright Countrywise Books,
Agricultural Press Limited 1973

ISBN 0 600 33537 2

Printed by Chapel River Press, Andover, England

Line drawings by Hayward Art Group

CONTENTS

Equipment, ingredients and rules

Please don't miss reading this chapter because the title is formidable. Cake-making is a pleasure, but it is also a science, and no successful cook will ignore the basic rules. Today's recipes are carefully and scientifically worked out, with skilfully balanced ingredients which will give an exact and excellent result.

The first and only rule of the cake-maker is follow the recipe; and that means in every detail, with the exact weights of the right ingredients, the right-sized tin, and the correct oven temperature.

Ingredients

Before cakes can be made successfully, the reasons for their possible failure must be understood, and the type and quality of ingredients used are of supreme importance.

Eggs: These give flavour, colour and volume to the cakes. Eggs should never be used straight from a refrigerator or there may be separation during mixing; they should be at room temperature. When eggs have to be separated, there must be no yolk left with the white or the fat from the yolk will lessen the volume of the beaten whites and change the texture.

Fats: These may be substituted for each other in baking, but results will vary considerably, particularly in flavour. *Butter* gives a delicious and distinct flavour, and unsalted or sweet butter gives the most delicate flavour. *Margarine* is cheap and easy to use, and will give a good light texture, but a different flavour. *Vegetable fats* give light, spongy cakes with good volume and a bland flavour, but special recipes created for them should be used as they contain air in place of the water in butter, and in substituting weight for weight 15 to 20 per cent less vegetable fat is needed than butter. *Lard* will cut easily into flour and give a flaky texture which is excellent for biscuits and pastry.

Sugar: This comes in a variety of forms, and these are rarely interchangeable in cake-making as they differ in sweetening power. *Castor sugar* is best for cake-making because its fine grains cream most easily. *Brown sugar* in gingerbreads and some fruit cakes will give a rich flavour and a darker cake. *Honey* gives a delicious flavour, but should not be used entirely in place of sugar in a recipe (no more than $\frac{1}{3}$ of the weight of sugar), or too great browning will result; a little bicarbonate of soda in honey-based cakes helps to neutralise the acidity of honey. *Treacle* gives a good flavour and special texture to gingerbread and some biscuits; golden syrup is blander and lighter, while black treacle has a very strong flavour.

Flour: *Plain flour* should always be used unless otherwise specified, and is particularly important in rich recipes which require little raising agent. *Self-raising flour* is useful for some cakes, but should not be used for pastry to which it gives a spongy texture. Keep all flours in a cool, dry place.

Raising agents: *Baking powder* consists of a combination of acid and alkaline ingredients which react together in moisture to form a gas which makes tiny bubbles in dough or batter; these expand quickly in baking and are set by the heat to form a light textured cake. *Bicarbonate of soda* is used to neutralise the acid in recipes containing sour milk, honey, treacle or spice, and gives a tender cake. *Yeast* is used for bread doughs, and is set to work by blending with a little liquid or sugar. Dried yeast comes in granular form and may be stored for some months, and directions for using it should be followed carefully.

Equipment

It is not necessary to buy a lot of expensive equipment for cake-making, but the right type of mixing and baking utensils will produce the best results.

Mixer: A wire whisk, rotary beater or electric mixer will all give good results. An over-beaten cake will have a poor texture, but for those who want to combine speed and skill a hand electric mixer is very satisfactory as it is so easily controlled. Thin wire beaters incorporate air best.

Tins: *Sandwich tins* should be bought in pairs; most recipes call for 7- or 8-inch tins. *Round cake tins* are most useful in 7- and 10-inch sizes; removable bottoms help in taking out the finished cake, but spring-form cake tins are better still, in which the sides split into two parts leaving the cake on the bottom of the tin, and they are particularly important for large light-textured cakes. *Tube tins* are decorative and useful for making babas and party sponge cakes. A plain round tube tin is useful in a 7-inch size, and a larger fluted tube tin is a pleasant luxury for making angel cakes and Continental yeast cakes. *Square and rectangular tins* are useful for gingerbreads, fruit cakes and rich sponge cakes which are to be cut in pieces. *Small patty tins* with plain round bases are needed for small tarts and cakes; shell-shaped indentations are important for Madeleines and for small sponges and queen cakes. *Loaf tins* are not only useful for bread but for fruit cakes and sweet cake-breads.

Foil: Aluminium foil may be used to make emergency cake tins of different sizes, or unusual shapes for party cakes.

Paper: *Greaseproof paper* is essential for lining cake tins. *Small paper cases* can be used for ease of baking and handling small cakes. *Thick plain white paper* should be used to line tins for certain types of meringues and biscuits. *Brown paper* should be used to cover rich cakes to prevent burning, and to tie round the outside of tins in which cakes are to have long cooking.

The oven

Exact temperatures and cooking times are essential to good cake-making. The oven should be heated and the control switch set to the required temperature at least 15 minutes before the cake is ready to go into the oven. It is worth having an oven temperature tested occasionally. As the years go by, ovens tend to 'run hot' and the thermometer may not be correct.

Methods

Creaming: Fat should be at room temperature before creaming. If fat is oily, it will prevent the proper incorporation of air into the batter. Fat and sugar should be creamed until soft, fluffy and pale.

Beating: Eggs should be beaten lightly. Cream of tartar added to egg whites gives a soft stable foam. A little sugar beaten into egg whites early in the mixing of the meringues reduces volume slightly, but gives a much more upstanding foam when the remaining sugar is folded in. When egg whites are beaten alone, the bowl and beater must be absolutely free from grease. Stiffness of whites may be tested by watching the rate of flow when the bowl is tipped. The traditional test of the inverted bowl means that the whites are in fact a little too dry and are over-beaten if they do not move.

Folding: A spatula is most often used to fold in mixtures. First use a sharp clean action as though cutting a cake, then with a lifting motion bring the heavier substance from the bottom of the bowl; repeat these slicing and lifting motions, turning the bowl as folding continues. Always fold the lighter into the heavier mixture. Flour is folded into creamed mixtures so that the air is not pressed out.

Testing the mixture: Sometimes recipes specify a consistency to be aimed at in mixing. A *soft dropping consistency* means that the mixture should be too stiff to pour, but it should drop from the spoon without being shaken. A *stiff dropping consistency* means the mixture should be too soft and sticky to handle, but stiff enough to keep its shape when shaken from a spoon. A *soft dough* means the mixture should be as soft as possible without being sticky.

Baking: Use the oven temperature specified, and also the correct position in the oven. If in doubt, place the cake in the centre of the oven. The cooked cake should be well risen, a good colour, and feel firm and springy when pressed lightly with the fingers. A thin skewer or knife may be used to pierce the cake, and should come

out clean when the cake is cooked. Most types of cakes will shrink slightly from the edges of the tin when cooked. Don't be tempted to open the oven until cooking time is completed.

Cooling and storing: Leave a cake in the tin for 2 or 3 minutes before turning out. Some fruit cakes should be left for an hour, and some delicate cakes should be left to set firmly before removing from the tin. Cool completely on a wire rack. Store cakes in a tin with a well fitting lid. Rich fruit cakes which are to be stored for some time should be first wrapped in greaseproof paper.

What went wrong and why

Fruit cakes

Too dry: Not enough liquid, or not enough fat or sugar. Too much raising agent. Baked too long.

Hard crust outside, with uncooked patch in centre: Oven too hot, and cake baked too quickly. Too much liquid, particularly when combined with syrup in gingerbreads.

Burnt outside: Oven too hot, or cake baked on too high a shelf.

Sinking in the middle: Too much raising agent in rich cakes. Insufficient creaming. Too hot or too cool oven.

Fruit sinking to the bottom: Too much liquid or raising agent. Too heavy fruit (usually cherries). Insufficient creaming.

Cracks across top: Too small a tin. Too hot oven. Too much raising agent, and not enough liquid.

Texture with large holes: Too much raising agent. Uneven mixing of flour.

Close texture, and cake not risen well: Not enough raising agent, or not enough liquid. Insufficient creaming. Too cool oven.

Crumbling texture: Not enough egg to bind ingredients in rich cakes. Not enough liquid in plain cakes. Too much raising agent. Overbaking.

Sandwiches and sponges

Domed top: Insufficient beating. Too hot oven.

Hollow top: Too much raising agent. Too cool oven.

Close doughy texture, or damp streak at base: Too much liquid, or too little flour or raising agent, or too much sugar. In sandwich cakes, this may be insufficient creaming.

Over-baked outside, soft doughy centre: Too hot oven. Baked too high in oven.

Baked through but pale spots when baked: Too cool oven. Baked too low in oven. Insufficient beating, so sugar still undissolved before baking.

Sponges
Sticking to sides of tin, sticky and damp when cold: Slightly underbaked, needing 3–5 minutes longer.
Shallow and not risen: Insufficient beating. Oven too cool. Too little raising agent.
Wrinkling on top after baking: Tin too small. Slight underbaking.

Swiss rolls
Dark, with very crisp edges: Too hot oven. Over-baked.
Pale and flabby: Too cool oven. Baked too low in oven. Under-baked.
Thin and badly risen: Insufficient beating, so too little aeration.

Scones
Small volume: Too little raising agent. Too cool oven.
Tough and leathery, too smooth and shiny: Over-kneading.
Too rough and shapeless: Under-kneading.
Hard and close-textured: Too little liquid.
Pale and doughy: Under-baked. Too cool oven. Baked too low in oven.

Yeast buns
Coarse-textured. Poor flavour: Dough not left long enough to ferment. Over-proving causing very open texture.
Small volume: Insufficiently proved, or too little liquid used in ferment. Badly over-proved, causing collapse in structure.
Thin and spreading: Too much liquid used in ferment. Over-proving causing collapse. Too cool oven.
Very dark. Burnt underneath: Too hot oven. Over-baking.
Pale and doughy: Too cool oven. Baked too low in oven. Under-baking.

Notes for American users

In the recipes in this book the ingredients are given in American standard cup measures as well as in Imperial measures. The list below gives some American equivalents or substitutes for terms used in the book.

British	American
Pudding basin	Pudding mold/ ovenproof bowl
Biscuit cutter	Cookie cutter
Castor sugar	Fine granulated sugar
Cake tin	Cake pan
Cocktail stick	Wooden toothpick
Deep cake tin	Spring form pan
Flan tin	Pie pan
Fresh yeast	Compressed yeast
Frying pan	Skillet
Greaseproof paper	Wax paper
Grill	Broil/broiler
Icing sugar	Confectioners' sugar
Marzipan	Almond paste
Palette knife	Spatula
Pastry case	Pie shell
Pie plate	Pie pan
Ring tin	Tube pan
Sandwich cake	Layer cake
Sandwich/sponge tin	Layer cake pan
Swiss roll tin	Jelly roll pan
Short pastry	Plain pastry

Notes for Australian users

Ingredients in this book are given in both cup measures and in pounds and ounces. In Australia the American 8-oz. measuring cup is used in conjunction with the Imperial pint of 20 fluid ounces. It is most important to remember that the Australian tablespoon differs from both the British and American tablespoon; the table below gives a comparison between the standard table-spoons used in the three countries. A teaspoon holds approximately 5 millilitres in all three countries; the British standard tablespoon holds 17·7 millilitres, the American 14·2 millilitres, and the Australian 20 millilitres.

British	American	Australian
1 teaspoon	1 teaspoon	1 teaspoon
1 tablespoon	1 tablespoon	1 tablespoon
2 tablespoons	3 tablespoons	2 tablespoons
3½ tablespoons	4 tablespoons	3 tablespoons
4 tablespoons	5 tablespoons	3½ tablespoons

All cup and spoon measures in this book are level.

SPONGE CAKES

Sponge cake making is a mystery to many otherwise good cooks, and though the best sponge cake makers seem to be born (like pastry makers), there are certain basic rules which should produce a satisfactory cake.

A sponge is fatless, while a sandwich contains fat. The exception to this definition is a Genoese sponge which is enriched by a small quantity of melted fat to improve flavour and keeping quality. A sponge rises without a raising agent, and its rising depends chiefly upon the amount of air whisked into the mixture. Air must always be retained in the batter when mixing sponge cakes, and flour should be sifted, then folded in gently. A sponge will stale fairly quickly and should be eaten within two days, but a sandwich will keep up to a week.

Both sponges and sandwiches should rise evenly, with level, not domed tops. They should have an even texture, not too close nor too open. Castor sugar should be used with both, because it dissolves more easily with the egg in a sponge, and will cream better in a sandwich.

Tins must be prepared very carefully for these cakes. A light sponge needs to be removed easily from the tin without breaking, so the tin should be brushed with melted fat, then dusted with flour. A sandwich tin should be brushed with melted fat, then a round of greaseproof paper laid in the bottom for ease of removal. A sheet of greaseproof paper should also be put on a greased Swiss roll tin, so that the underside of the sponge remains moist and pliable for rolling.

In these days of electric mixers, it is important that cakes should not be over-beaten. When a mixture is to be beaten over hot water, the bowl should not be allowed to touch the water or the mixture will become too hot and the eggs will 'set' so that they don't mix well with the sugar and will not hold air.

Simple sponge cake

Cooking time: 20 minutes

Temperature: 400°F., 200°C., Gas Mark 6

Imperial	Metric	American
4 eggs	4 eggs	4 eggs
4 oz. castor sugar	100 g. castor sugar	$\frac{1}{2}$ cup granulated sugar
pinch salt	pinch salt	pinch salt
4 oz. plain flour	100 g. plain flour	1 cup all-purpose flour

Put the eggs and sugar in a bowl and whisk with a pinch of salt until the mixture is light, thick and creamy. Sift the flour on to the mixture and fold in lightly using a metal spoon. Put the mixture into two greased and floured sandwich tins, and bake for 20 minutes. The cake will show signs of shrinking from the edge of the tin when ready.

Genoese sponge

Cooking time: 45 minutes

Temperature: 400°F., 200°C., Gas Mark 6

Imperial	Metric	American
4 eggs	4 eggs	4 eggs
4 oz. castor sugar	100 g. castor sugar	½ cup granulated sugar
3 oz. flour	75 g. flour	¾ cup flour
3 oz. butter, melted	75 g. butter, melted	6 tablespoons melted butter

Beat the eggs and sugar over hot, but not boiling, water until light and thick. Sift the flour. Melt the butter over gentle heat, but do not make it hot. Remove basin from heat and continue beating for 3 minutes. Fold in half the flour and the melted butter very gently. Fold in the remaining flour, avoiding stirring as much as possible. Put into a prepared 8-inch (20-cm.) sandwich tin and bake for 45 minutes. This cake may be baked in a rectangular tin, and cut into pieces for making small fancy cakes. A firmer texture, which will be easier to handle, is achieved by adding an extra 1½ oz. flour.

Victoria sandwich

Cooking time: 30 minutes

Temperature: 325°F., 170°C., Gas Mark 3

Imperial	Metric	American
4 oz. margarine	100 g. margarine	½ cup margarine
4 oz. castor sugar	100 g. castor sugar	½ cup granulated sugar
2 eggs	2 eggs	2 eggs
4 oz. self-raising flour	100 g. self-raising flour	1 cup all-purpose flour sifted with 1 teaspoon baking powder

Cream the margarine and sugar together until light and fluffy and almost white. Add the eggs one at a time and beat well. Fold in the sifted flour, and put mixture into two prepared 7-inch (18-cm.) sandwich tins. Bake for 30 minutes. Leave in tins for 2 minutes, then cool on a wire tray. Spread with jam or cream, and ice if desired.

Cornflour sponge

Cooking time: 20 minutes

Temperature: 375°F., 190°C., Gas Mark 5

Imperial	Metric	American
3 eggs	3 eggs	3 eggs
3 oz. castor sugar	75 g. castor sugar	6 tablespoons castor sugar
3 oz. plain flour	75 g. plain flour	¾ cup all-purpose flour
1 oz. cornflour	25 g. cornflour	¼ cup cornstarch
1 teaspoon baking powder	1 teaspoon baking powder	1 teaspoon baking powder
pinch salt	pinch salt	pinch salt
1 oz. butter	25 g. butter	2 tablespoons butter
3 tablespoons hot water	3 tablespoons hot water	¼ cup hot water

Whisk the eggs and sugar until light and fluffy and very pale in colour. Fold in the flour sifted with the cornflour, baking powder, and salt. Lastly fold in the fat, melted in the hot water. Put into two 7-inch (18-cm.) sandwich tins. Bake for 20 minutes.

Swiss roll

Cooking time: 10 minutes

Temperature: 400°F., 200°C.,
Gas Mark 6

Imperial	Metric	American
3 eggs	3 eggs	3 eggs
4½ oz. castor sugar	125 g. castor sugar	½ cup plus 1 tablespoon granulated sugar
3 oz. plain flour	75 g. plain flour	¾ cup all-purpose flour
½ teaspoon baking powder	½ teaspoon baking powder	½ teaspoon baking powder
1 tablespoon cold water	1 tablespoon cold water	1 tablespoon cold water

Beat the eggs and sugar until very light and fluffy, and fold in the flour sifted with baking powder, and the cold water. Spread the mixture evenly in a greased and lined tin, and bake for 10 minutes. Turn out on to sugared paper, trim edges. spread quickly with warm jam and roll up tightly. Finish with·a sprinkling of castor sugar.

Sponge drops

Cooking time: 5 minutes

Temperature: 450°F., 230°C.,
Gas Mark 8

Imperial	Metric	American
2 eggs	2 eggs	2 eggs
pinch salt	pinch salt	pinch salt
3 oz. castor sugar	75 g. castor sugar	6 tablespoons granulated sugar
3 oz. plain flour	75 g. plain flour	¾ cup all-purpose flour
¼ teaspoon baking powder	¼ teaspoon baking powder	¼ teaspoon baking powder

Separate the egg yolks and whites. Add the salt to whites and whisk until very stiff. Gradually whisk in the sugar and egg yolks alternately until the mixture is thick and creamy. Fold in the flour sifted with baking powder, and put in spoonfuls on greased and floured baking sheets. Dust with sugar and bake for 5 minutes. Cool and sandwich together with raspberry jam and whipped cream, dusting with icing sugar.

FRUIT CAKES

Fruit cake is always popular, and few housewives like to be without one in the tin. In this chapter will be found recipes varying from the light currant 'luncheon' cake to the heavily fruited celebration cake, suitable for eating at almost any hour of the day, and good for lunch-boxes and picnics.

When a cake needs long baking, there is a danger that the crust will be hard and dry, so a strip of corrugated paper, or double brown paper or newspaper round the outside of the tin will help to prevent this. The cake should also stand on several thicknesses of paper on a baking sheet, and the top may be protected with brown paper when it has become golden and firm. This paper method should only be used when a cool oven is required. The middle shelf of the oven is the best place for all large cakes, because there the heat is more evenly distributed.

To test a cake to see if it is baked, press it lightly with the finger at the centre of the top while still in the oven. If the top is firm, the cake is cooked. A cake may also be tested with a skewer or knife, which will come out clean when the cake is cooked. A cake will also begin to shrink from the sides of the tin when it is done. A rich fruit cake will 'sing' in the oven, and if there is a slight hissing sound, it is not yet ready to take out.

Dundee cake

Cooking time: 2½ hours

Temperature: 325°F., 170°C., Gas Mark 3

Illustrated on page 19

Imperial	Metric	American
8 oz. butter	225 g. butter	1 cup butter
8 oz. castor sugar	225 g. castor sugar	1 cup granulated sugar
5 eggs	5 eggs	5 eggs
8 oz. self-raising flour	225 g. self-raising flour	2 cups all-purpose flour sifted with 2 teaspoons baking powder
½ teaspoon nutmeg	½ teaspoon nutmeg	½ teaspoon nutmeg
12 oz. mixed currants and sultanas	350 g. mixed currants and sultanas	2¼ cups mixed currants and white raisins
3 oz. glacé cherries, chopped	75 g. glacé cherries, chopped	⅓ cup chopped candied cherries
2 oz. chopped candied peel	50 g. chopped candied peel	⅓ cup chopped candied peel
3 oz. ground almonds	75 g. ground almonds	¾ cup ground almonds
2 oz. split blanched almonds	50 g. split blanched almonds	½ cup split blanched almonds

Cream the butter and sugar until light and fluffy, and add the eggs one at a time with a sprinkling of flour to prevent the mixture curdling. Beat well after each addition. Stir in most of the flour and lastly the fruit lightly coated with the rest of the flour, and the ground almonds. Turn into a buttered and lined 10-inch (25-cm.) deep round cake tin; smooth the top and arrange the blanched split almonds on it. Bake for 2½ hours.

Variation

Omit nuts from the top of the cake and when cooked and cooled brush top with egg white. Roll out ½ lb. marzipan into a 10-inch (25-cm.) round and place on top of the cake. Score with a criss cross pattern, brush again with egg white and place under the grill to brown (illustrated on page 19).

Keeping cake

Cooking time: 4 hours

Temperature: 300°F., 150°C., Gas Mark 2

Imperial	Metric	American
8 oz. butter	225 g. butter	1 cup butter
8 oz. soft brown or castor sugar	225 g. soft brown or castor sugar	1 cup soft brown or granulated sugar
1 tablespoon black treacle	1 tablespoon black treacle	1 tablespoon molasses
4 eggs	4 eggs	4 eggs
4 tablespoons cold tea or sherry or brandy	4 tablespoons cold tea or sherry or brandy	$\frac{1}{3}$ cup cold tea or sherry or brandy
grated rind of 1 lemon	grated rind of 1 lemon	grated rind of 1 lemon
$\frac{1}{2}$ teaspoon vanilla essence	$\frac{1}{2}$ teaspoon vanilla essence	$\frac{1}{2}$ teaspoon vanilla extract
4 oz. self-raising flour	100 g. self-raising flour	$2\frac{1}{2}$ cups all-purpose flour sifted with 2 teaspoons baking powder
6 oz. plain flour	175 g. plain flour	
$\frac{1}{4}$ teaspoon salt	$\frac{1}{4}$ teaspoon salt	$\frac{1}{4}$ teaspoon salt
1 teaspoon mixed spice	1 teaspoon mixed spice	1 teaspoon mixed spice
pinch cinnamon	pinch cinnamon	pinch cinnamon
pinch nutmeg	pinch nutmeg	pinch nutmeg
12 oz. currants	350 g. currants	$2\frac{1}{4}$ cups currants
12 oz. sultanas	350 g. sultanas	$2\frac{1}{4}$ cups white raisins
8 oz. stoned raisins	225 g. stoned raisins	$1\frac{1}{2}$ cups seedless raisins
2 oz. chopped candied peel	50 g. chopped candied peel	$\frac{1}{3}$ cup chopped candied peel
2 oz. chopped almonds	50 g. chopped almonds	$\frac{1}{2}$ cup chopped almonds
2 oz. glacé cherries, halved	50 g. glacé cherries, halved	$\frac{1}{4}$ cup halved candied cherries

Cream the butter and sugar until light and fluffy. Lightly mix together the black treacle, eggs, tea, lemon rind and vanilla essence. Sift together the flours and spices. Add treacle mixture and flour mixture alternately to the creamed mixture, but do not beat. Add all the remaining ingredients and just stir enough to mix them together. Put into a greased 10-inch (25-cm.) deep round cake tin lined with two thicknesses of paper; leave for an hour to stand, then bake for 4 hours. This is an ideal Christmas cake, which stores for many months in a tin, and is also an excellent cake for picnics.

George Washington cake

Cooking time: 1 hour

Temperature: 350°F., 180°C., Gas Mark 4

Imperial	Metric	American
4 eggs	4 eggs	4 eggs
1 lb. butter	450 g. butter	2 cups butter
$1\frac{1}{2}$ lb. sugar	700 g. sugar	3 cups sugar
1 lb. plain flour	450 g. plain flour	4 cups all-purpose flour
1 tablespoon baking powder	1 tablespoon baking powder	1 tablespoon baking powder
1 teaspoon mace	1 teaspoon mace	1 teaspoon mace
1 teaspoon cinnamon	1 teaspoon cinnamon	1 teaspoon cinnamon
1 teaspoon salt	1 teaspoon salt	1 teaspoon salt
$\frac{1}{3}$ pint milk	2 dl. milk	$\frac{3}{4}$ cup milk
6 oz. raisins	175 g. raisins	1 cup raisins
3 oz. currants	75 g. currants	$\frac{1}{2}$ cup currants
2 oz. chopped candied peel	50 g. chopped candied peel	$\frac{1}{3}$ cup chopped candied peel

Separate the eggs. Cream the butter and sugar and add the egg yolks. Sift the flour, baking powder and spices and add alternately with the milk, beating well. Stir in the raisins, currants and peel; then fold in stiffly beaten egg whites. Pour into a buttered 10-inch (25-cm.) deep round cake tin, and bake for 1 hour. Cool in tin for 10 minutes before turning out. This cake is very good with a soft white icing.

1881 Currant cake

Cooking time: 1¾ hours

Temperature: 325°F., 170°C., Gas Mark 3

Imperial	Metric	American
8 oz. butter	225 g. butter	1 cup butter
1 lb. sugar	450 g. sugar	2 cups sugar
3 eggs	3 eggs	3 eggs
12 oz. black treacle	350 g. black treacle	1 cup molasses
½ pint milk	3 dl. milk	1¼ cups milk
1¼ lb. plain flour	550 g. plain flour	5 cups all-purpose flour
3 teaspoons baking powder	3 teaspoons baking powder	3 teaspoons baking powder
1 teaspoon salt	1 teaspoon salt	1 teaspoon salt
1 teaspoon cinnamon	1 teaspoon cinnamon	1 teaspoon cinnamon
1 teaspoon ground cloves	1 teaspoon ground cloves	1 teaspoon ground cloves
1 teaspoon nutmeg	1 teaspoon nutmeg	1 teaspoon nutmeg
1 lb. currants	450 g. currants	4 cups currants

Cream the butter and sugar. Beat the eggs into the treacle and blend into creamed mixture. Sift the flour, baking powder, salt and spices. Add the flour mixture and milk alternately to the creamed mixture, and finally stir in the currants. Put into a 12-inch (30-cm.) square cake tin and bake for 1¾ hours.

Chocolate nut cake

Cooking time: 1¼ hours

Temperature: 375°F., 190°C., Gas Mark 5

Imperial	Metric	American
4 oz. plain flour	100 g. plain flour	1 cup all-purpose flour
½ teaspoon baking powder	½ teaspoon baking powder	½ teaspoon baking powder
pinch salt	pinch salt	pinch salt
5½ oz. castor sugar	150 g. castor sugar	⅔ cup granulated sugar
4 oz. dates	100 g. dates	⅔ cup dates
8 oz. Brazil nut kernels	225 g. Brazil nut kernels	2 cups Brazil nut kernels
2 oz. glacé cherries	50 g. glacé cherries	¼ cup candied cherries
4 oz. chocolate chips	100 g. chocolate chips	⅔ cup chocolate chips
3 eggs	3 eggs	3 eggs

Sieve together the flour, baking powder and salt, and mix with the sugar. Add the chopped dates and nuts, together with the halved glacé cherries and the chocolate chips. Separate the eggs, beat the egg whites until light and frothy, fold in the yolks, and stir into the fruit and flour mixture. Put into a greased and lined small loaf tin. Bake for 1¼ hours.

School cake

Cooking time: 1½ hours

Temperature: 325°F., 170°C., Gas Mark 3

Imperial	Metric	American
1 lb. wholemeal flour	450 g. wholemeal flour	4 cups whole-wheat flour
12 oz. butter	350 g. butter	1½ cups butter
8 oz. mixed chopped nuts	225 g. mixed chopped nuts	2 cups mixed chopped nuts
12 oz. sultanas	350 g. sultanas	2½ cups white raisins
8 oz. honey	225 g. honey	⅔ cup honey
juice of 3 oranges	juice of 3 oranges	juice of 3 oranges
4 eggs	4 eggs	4 eggs

Sieve the flour and rub in the butter. Stir in the nuts and sultanas. Melt the honey, add to the orange juice, and pour into the dry mixture. Stir in the eggs and beat well. Put into a greased and lined 10-inch (25-cm.) deep round cake tin and bake for 1½ hours.

Uncooked fruit cake

Imperial	Metric	American
8 oz. marshmallows	225 g. marshmallows	8 oz. marshmallows
1½ lb. digestive biscuits	700 g. digestive biscuits	1½ lb. graham crackers
1 oz. angelica	25 g. angelica	1 oz. candied angelica leaves
3 tablespoons orange juice	3 tablespoons orange juice	¼ cup orange juice
10 tablespoons evaporated milk	2 dl. evaporated milk	¾ cup evaporated milk
½ teaspoon cinnamon	½ teaspoon cinnamon	½ teaspoon cinnamon
½ teaspoon nutmeg	½ teaspoon nutmeg	½ teaspoon nutmeg
¼ teaspoon ground cloves	¼ teaspoon ground cloves	¼ teaspoon ground cloves
12 oz. sultanas and raisins	350 g. sultanas and raisins	2¼ cups white and dark raisins
8 oz. chopped candied peel	225 g. chopped candied peel	1½ cups chopped candied peel
4 oz. glacé cherries	100 g. glacé cherries	½ cup candied cherries
4 oz. dates, chopped	100 g. dates, chopped	⅔ cup chopped dates
4 oz. walnuts	100 g. walnuts	1 cup walnuts

Chop the marshmallows with a pair of wet scissors. Crush the biscuits with a rolling pin. Chop the angelica finely. Leave the marshmallows to stand in the orange juice and milk for 20 minutes. Mix the spices, angelica, chopped fruit and nuts. Stir in the marshmallows and liquid, and finally the biscuit crumbs. Press very firmly into a lined 9-inch (23-cm.) round cake tin, cover with foil, and leave for 2 days before turning out and cutting. Store in refrigerator. This is an unusual cake, popular with children, and makes a useful second cake at Christmas time, when it can be topped with a little icing and decorated with whole glacé fruit and nuts.

Apple sauce cake

Cooking time: 40 minutes

Temperature: 350°F., 180°C., Gas Mark 4

Imperial	Metric	American
4 oz. butter	100 g. butter	½ cup butter
8 oz. sugar	225 g. sugar	2 cups sugar
½ pint cold unsweetened apple sauce	3 dl. cold unsweetened apple sauce	1¼ cups cold unsweetened applesauce
8 oz. plain flour	225 g. plain flour	2 cups all-purpose flour
½ teaspoon ground cloves	½ teaspoon ground cloves	½ teaspoon ground cloves
1 teaspoon cinnamon	1 teaspoon cinnamon	1 teaspoon cinnamon
1 teaspoon bicarbonate of soda	1 teaspoon bicarbonate of soda	1 teaspoon baking soda
6 oz. nuts and raisins, chopped	175 g. nuts and raisins, chopped	1 cup chopped nuts and raisins

Cream the butter and sugar until light and fluffy, and add apple sauce. Add the flour sifted with spices and soda, and then add the nuts and raisins. Put into a buttered 7-inch (18-cm.) deep round cake tin and bake for 40 minutes. This is an easy spicy cake.

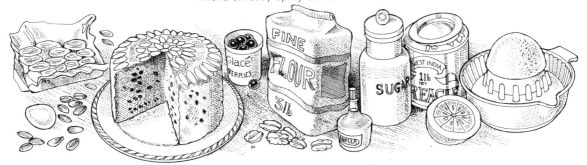

CUT AND COME AGAIN CAKES

This chapter concerns the easy, undemanding cakes which are useful for storing in the tin against all occasions. Some of these simple cakes may be sliced and buttered; others are equally good served plain with a cup of tea or coffee, or can be used to revive the old custom of a glass of wine and piece of a cake as a mid-morning restorative.

Fruit cakes, chocolate cakes, sponge cakes and small cakes will be found · in their respective chapters, but here are the simple spice and seed cakes, orange, honey and cherry cakes, which are light on the budget and always popular.

Honey loaf

Cooking time: 1¼ hours

Temperature: 350°F., 180°C.,
Gas Mark 4

Imperial	Metric	American
4 oz. butter	100 g. butter	½ cup butter
4 oz. castor sugar	100 g. castor sugar	½ cup granulated sugar
6 tablespoons honey	6 tablespoons honey	½ cup honey
1 egg	1 egg	1 egg
10½ oz. plain flour	300 g. plain flour	2⅔ cups all-purpose flour
3 teaspoons baking powder	3 teaspoons baking powder	3 teaspoons baking powder
1 teaspoon salt	1 teaspoon salt	1 teaspoon salt
¼ pint milk	1½ dl. milk	⅔ cup milk

Cream the butter and sugar until light and fluffy, and mix in the honey thoroughly. Beat in the egg. Sieve the flour, baking powder and salt, and stir into the creamed mixture alternately with the milk. Put into a buttered large loaf tin and bake for 1¼ hours. Cool, slice and spread with butter.

Sugar and spice cake

Cooking time: 1 hour

Temperature: 325°F., 170°C.,
Gas Mark 3

Imperial	Metric	American
4 oz. butter	100 g. butter	½ cup butter
6 oz. sugar	175 g. sugar	¾ cup sugar
2 eggs	2 eggs	2 eggs
4 tablespoons hot water	4 tablespoons hot water	⅓ cup hot water
10 oz. plain flour	275 g. plain flour	2½ cups all-purpose flour
1 teaspoon bicarbonate of soda	1 teaspoon bicarbonate of soda	1 teaspoon baking soda
8 oz. raspberry or apricot jam or orange marmalade	225 g. raspberry or apricot jam or orange marmalade	¾ cup raspberry or apricot jam or orange marmalade
1 teaspoon cinnamon	1 teaspoon cinnamon	1 teaspoon cinnamon
½ teaspoon mixed spice	½ teaspoon mixed spice	½ teaspoon mixed spice

Cream the butter and sugar until light and fluffy. Add the eggs one at a time, then the water. Sift the flour and soda together and then fold in alternately with the jam or marmalade and beat thoroughly to blend the ingredients. Put into a buttered 8-inch (20-cm.) deep round cake tin and bake for 1 hour. Turn out and cool, and if liked, ice with an orange glacé icing (see page 69).

Cherry cake

Cooking time: 1½ hours

Temperature: 325°F., 170°C.,
Gas Mark 3

Imperial	Metric	American
8 oz. plain flour	225 g. plain flour	2 cups all-purpose flour
1½ teaspoons baking powder	1½ teaspoons baking powder	1½ teaspoons baking powder
6 oz. butter	175 g. butter	¾ cup butter
6 oz. castor sugar	175 g. castor sugar	¾ cup sugar
3 eggs	3 eggs	3 eggs
grated rind of 2 lemons	grated rind of 2 lemons	grated rind of 2 lemons
1 tablespoon milk	1 tablespoon milk	1 tablespoon milk
4 oz. glacé cherries	100 g. glacé cherries	½ cup candied cherries

Sift the flour and baking powder. Cream the butter and sugar until light and fluffy. Work in the eggs one at a time; add the lemon rind. Fold in the flour and baking powder, then the milk. Lightly coat the cherries with flour and fold in. Put into a greased 7-inch (18-cm.) deep round cake tin and bake for 1½ hours.

Quick orange cake

Cooking time: 1¼ hours

Temperature: 350°F., 180°C.,
Gas Mark 4

Imperial	Metric	American
4 oz. butter	100 g. butter	½ cup butter
8 oz. sugar	225 g. sugar	1 cup sugar
⅓ pint orange juice	2 dl. orange juice	¾ cup orange juice
2 eggs	2 eggs	2 eggs
8 oz. plain flour	225 g. plain flour	2 cups all-purpose flour
4 teaspoons baking powder	4 teaspoons baking powder	4 teaspoons baking powder
¼ teaspoon salt	¼ teaspoon salt	¼ teaspoon salt
Topping:	**Topping:**	**Topping:**
grated rind of 2 oranges	grated rind of 2 oranges	grated rind of 2 oranges
3 tablespoons castor sugar	3 tablespoons castor sugar	¼ cup granulated sugar

Melt the butter, and pour the hot butter on to the sugar, then stir in the orange juice and beaten eggs. Add the flour, baking powder and salt and beat well. Pour into a greased 8-inch (20-cm.) deep round cake tin and sprinkle with a mixture of grated orange rind and sugar. Bake for 1¼ hours.

Walnut loaf

Cooking time: 1¼ hours

Temperature: 350°F., 180°C.,
Gas Mark 4

Imperial	Metric	American
12 oz. plain flour	350 g. plain flour	3 cups all-purpose flour
4 teaspoons baking powder	4 teaspoons baking powder	4 teaspoons baking powder
¾ teaspoon salt	¾ teaspoon salt	¾ teaspoon salt
8 oz. sugar	225 g. sugar	1 cup sugar
4 oz. walnuts, chopped	100 g. walnuts, chopped	1 cup chopped walnuts
2 eggs	2 eggs	2 eggs
½ pint milk	3 dl. milk	1¼ cups milk
2 tablespoons melted butter	2 tablespoons melted butter	3 tablespoons melted butter

Sieve together the flour, baking powder and salt. Stir in the sugar and walnuts; then mix with the beaten eggs, milk and melted butter. Put into a buttered large loaf tin and leave to stand for 20 minutes. Bake for 1¼ hours. Cool, slice and spread with butter and honey.

Madeira cake

Cooking time: 1 hour

Temperature: 350°F., 180°C., Gas Mark 4

Imperial	Metric	American
4 oz. butter	100 g. butter	$\frac{1}{2}$ cup butter
4 oz. castor sugar	100 g. castor sugar	$\frac{1}{2}$ cup granulated sugar
8 oz. plain flour	225 g. plain flour	2 cups all-purpose flour
2 oz. ground rice	50 g. ground rice	$\frac{1}{3}$ cup rice flour
1 teaspoon cream of tartar	1 teaspoon cream of tartar	1 teaspoon cream of tartar
1 teaspoon bicarbonate of soda	1 teaspoon bicarbonate of soda	1 teaspoon baking soda
$\frac{1}{4}$ teaspoon salt	$\frac{1}{4}$ teaspoon salt	$\frac{1}{4}$ teaspoon salt
grated rind and juice of $\frac{1}{2}$ lemon	grated rind and juice of $\frac{1}{2}$ lemon	grated rind and juice of $\frac{1}{2}$ lemon
4 eggs	4 eggs	4 eggs

Cream the butter and sugar, and work in the flour, ground rice, cream of tartar, soda and salt. Add the lemon rind and juice. Separate the eggs and beat the egg whites until stiff. Add the yolks and whites to the mixture. Put into a buttered 7-inch (18-cm.) deep round cake tin, and bake for 1 hour. Just before the cake is finished, put two slices of candied peel on top.

Seed cake

Cooking time: 1 hour

Temperature: 350°F., 180°C., Gas Mark 4

Imperial	Metric	American
1 lb. plain flour	450 g. plain flour	4 cups all-purpose flour
1 teaspoon baking powder	1 teaspoon baking powder	1 teaspoon baking powder
1 oz. caraway seeds	25 g. caraway seeds	3 tablespoons caraway seeds
6 oz. butter	175 g. butter	$\frac{3}{4}$ cup butter
8 oz. sugar	225 g. sugar	1 cup sugar
3 eggs	3 eggs	3 eggs

Sift the flour and baking powder and stir in the caraway seeds. Cream the butter and sugar and work in well-beaten eggs. Add the flour mixture gradually and beat well. Beat for 5 minutes, then put into a buttered 7-inch (18-cm.) deep round cake tin and bake for 1 hour.

GINGERBREADS

Gingerbread can take many different forms. There are the light spongy kinds, the rich heavy sticky ones, and the biscuit-like gingerbreads which are so suitable for lunchboxes and picnics. A square of gingerbread is good served with a spoonful of whipped cream; it is also delicious with sweetened apple sauce and cream. Gingerbread mixtures can be poured over fresh or tinned fruit and baked as upside-down cakes. A wedge of gingerbread and a hunk of cheese is a delicious snack.

Syrup or treacle are essential for most gingerbreads. Care must be taken in baking, since mixtures containing syrup burn quickly if the oven is too hot, and a slow to moderate oven is normally used. The flavour of gingerbread is improved by a little ground cloves, nutmeg and cinnamon added to the ground ginger in the recipe. The richer gingerbreads improve with keeping, and should be kept in a tin or bread bin for a few days before cutting.

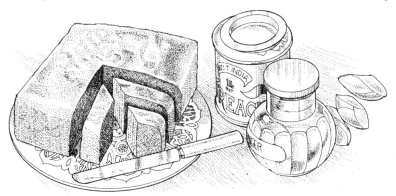

Parkin

Cooking time: 1 hour

Temperature: 350°F., 180°C., Gas Mark 4

Imperial	Metric	American
6 oz. plain flour	175 g. plain flour	1½ cups all-purpose flour
1 teaspoon salt	1 teaspoon salt	1 teaspoon salt
1 teaspoon ground ginger	1 teaspoon ground ginger	1 teaspoon ground ginger
2 teaspoons cinnamon	2 teaspoons cinnamon	2 teaspoons cinnamon
1 teaspoon bicarbonate of soda	1 teaspoon bicarbonate of soda	1 teaspoon baking soda
10 oz. oatmeal or rolled oats	275 g. oatmeal or rolled oats	1⅔ cups ground oatmeal or 3 cups rolled oats
6 oz. black treacle	175 g. black treacle	½ cup molasses
5 oz. butter	125 g. butter	⅔ cup butter
4 oz. soft brown sugar	100 g. soft brown sugar	½ cup soft brown sugar
¼ pint milk	1½ dl. milk	⅔ cup milk
1 egg	1 egg	1 egg

Sift together the flour, salt, spices and soda. Add the oatmeal, and toss lightly to mix. Warm the treacle, butter, sugar and milk until the butter has melted. Cool slightly, add the egg and beat well. Pour into the centre of the dry ingredients and stir rapidly until smooth. Turn into a greased and lined 7-inch (18-cm.) square tin. Bake in the centre of the oven for 1 hour. This is the traditional cake to eat for Guy Fawkes celebrations, and should be stored in an airtight tin for a couple of weeks before using.

17

Sour milk gingerbread

Cooking time: 30 minutes

Temperature: 325°F., 170°C.,
Gas Mark 3

Imperial	Metric	American
12 oz. golden syrup or black treacle	350 g. golden syrup or black treacle	1 cup golden syrup or molasses
3 oz. butter	75 g. butter	6 tablespoons butter
1½ teaspoons bicarbonate of soda	1½ teaspoons bicarbonate of soda	1½ teaspoons baking soda
8 oz. plain flour	225 g. plain flour	2 cups all-purpose flour
2 teaspoons ground ginger	2 teaspoons ground ginger	2 teaspoons ground ginger
½ teaspoon salt	½ teaspoon salt	½ teaspoon salt
1 egg	1 egg	1 egg
6 tablespoons sour milk	6 tablespoons sour milk	½ cup sour milk

Heat the syrup or treacle with the butter until the butter melts. Add the bicarbonate of soda and beat hard. Mix together the flour, ginger and salt, pour on the syrup mixture, and beat to a smooth batter with the egg and sour milk. Pour into a greased 8- by 12-inch (20- by 30-cm.) tin and bake for 30 minutes.

Coventry gingerbread

Cooking time: 30 minutes

Temperature: 325°F., 170°C.,
Gas Mark 3

Imperial	Metric	American
6 oz. wholemeal flour	175 g. wholemeal flour	1½ cups whole-wheat flour
3 oz. castor sugar	75 g. castor sugar	6 tablespoons granulated sugar
1 teaspoon ground ginger	1 teaspoon ground ginger	1 teaspoon ground ginger
4 oz. butter	100 g. butter	½ cup butter
2 oz. crystallised ginger	50 g. crystallised ginger	⅓ cup candied ginger

Sift together the flour, sugar and ginger. Rub in the butter lightly, then add the chopped crystallised ginger. Press the mixture very lightly into a greased 7-inch (18-cm.) sandwich tin, and bake for 30 minutes. Remove from the tin to cool, and break into pieces to serve.

Ginger jumbles

Cooking time: 10 minutes

Temperature: 350°F., 180°C.,
Gas Mark 4

Imperial	Metric	American
4 oz. butter	100 g. butter	½ cup butter
4 oz. castor sugar	100 g. castor sugar	½ cup granulated sugar
1 egg	1 egg	1 egg
10 oz. plain flour	275 g. plain flour	2½ cups all-purpose flour
1 teaspoon baking powder	1 teaspoon baking powder	1 teaspoon baking powder
1 teaspoon ground ginger	1 teaspoon ground ginger	1 teaspoon ground ginger
glacé icing	glacé icing	glacé icing
crystallised ginger	crystallised ginger	candied ginger

Cream the butter and sugar until the mixture is fluffy. Add the egg, then work in the flour sieved with the baking powder and ginger. Make a firm dough and roll out into long sausage shapes about ½ inch thick. Cut into lengths and form these into 'S' shapes. Bake for 10 minutes. Cool on a wire rack, then decorate with glacé icing (see page 69) and chopped ginger.

Dundee cake (page 10), and giant currant cookies (page 68)

Chocolate ginger cake

Cooking time: 30 minutes

Temperature: 375°F., 190°C.,
   Gas Mark 5

Imperial	Metric	American
6 oz. self-raising flour	175 g. self-raising flour	1½ cups all-purpose flour sifted with 1½ teaspoons baking powder
3 teaspoons ground ginger	3 teaspoons ground ginger	3 teaspoons ground ginger
6 oz. butter	175 g. butter	¾ cup butter
5 oz. soft brown sugar	125 g. soft brown sugar	⅔ cup soft brown sugar
3 eggs	3 eggs	3 eggs
whipped cream or thick custard	whipped cream or thick custard	whipped cream or thick custard
Icing:	**Icing:**	**Icing:**
3 oz. plain chocolate	75 g. plain chocolate	½ cup semi-sweet chocolate pieces
2 tablespoons water	2 tablespoons water	3 tablespoons water
½ oz. butter	15 g. butter	1 tablespoon butter
8 oz. icing sugar	225 g. icing sugar	1¾ cups confectioners' sugar

Sieve together the flour and ground ginger. Cream the butter with the sugar and work in the eggs, one at a time. Fold in the flour and put into two greased 8-inch (20-cm.) sandwich tins. Bake for 30 minutes. Cool on a wire tray and sandwich together with whipped cream or thick custard. Make the icing by melting together over hot water the chocolate, water and butter. Cool and gradually beat in the icing sugar, pour it over the cake and decorate with nuts or pieces of crystallised ginger.

Apple gingerbread

Cooking time: 40 minutes

Temperature: 350°F., 180°C.,
   Gas Mark 4

Imperial	Metric	American
1 large cooking apple	1 large cooking apple	1 large cooking apple
6 cloves	6 cloves	6 cloves
2 teaspoons sugar	2 teaspoons sugar	2 teaspoons sugar
3 tablespoons water	3 tablespoons water	3 tablespoons water
6 oz. self-raising flour	175 g. self-raising flour	1½ cups all-purpose flour sifted with 1½ teaspoons baking powder
2 teaspoons ground ginger	2 teaspoons ground ginger	2 teaspoons ground ginger
3 oz. sugar	75 g. sugar	6 tablespoons sugar
1 egg	1 egg	1 egg
4 oz. black treacle	100 g. black treacle	⅓ cup molasses
3 oz. butter, melted	75 g. butter, melted	6 tablespoons melted butter
Fudge icing:	**Fudge icing:**	**Fudge icing:**
1 oz. butter	25 g. butter	2 tablespoons butter
2 oz. black treacle	50 g. black treacle	3 tablespoons molasses
2 oz. icing sugar	50 g. icing sugar	½ cup confectioners' sugar
pinch cinnamon	pinch cinnamon	pinch cinnamon

Peel, core and slice the apple, and put into a saucepan with the cloves, sugar and water. Cook until tender, remove the cloves and mash the apple with a fork. Leave to cool. Put the flour and ginger into a bowl and stir in the sugar. Add the cooked apple, beaten egg, black treacle and butter and beat well together. Turn into a medium loaf tin and bake for 40 minutes. Make the icing by creaming together the butter, treacle and sugar until light and fluffy. Add the cinnamon, and spread the icing on the cake. Decorate with a scattering of chopped nuts or chopped crystallised ginger.

Gingerbread upside-down cake

Cooking time: see recipe

Temperature: see recipe

Imperial	Metric	American
1 oz. butter	25 g. butter	2 tablespoons butter
1 oz. brown sugar	25 g. brown sugar	2 tablespoons brown sugar
8 pear halves (or pineapple rings or apple slices)	8 pear halves (or pineapple rings or apple slices)	8 pear halves (or pineapple rings or apple slices)
gingerbread mixture	gingerbread mixture	gingerbread mixture

Melt the butter in a heavy pan, add the sugar and stir until syrupy. Pour into a buttered baking tin, and arrange the fruit hollow side down in the syrup. Pour over any plain gingerbread mixture and bake for time given for the gingerbread. Loosen the edges and turn out on a serving dish. Serve warm or cold with or without cream.

Danish Christmas gingerbread

Cooking time: 1 hour

Temperature: 375°F., 190°C., Gas Mark 5

Imperial	Metric	American
1 lb. honey	450 g. honey	$1\frac{1}{3}$ cups honey
6 oz. butter	175 g. butter	$\frac{3}{4}$ cup butter
6 oz. castor sugar	175 g. castor sugar	$\frac{3}{4}$ cup sugar
1 oz. ground ginger	25 g. ground ginger	$\frac{1}{4}$ cup ground ginger
1 teaspoon cinnamon	1 teaspoon cinnamon	1 teaspoon cinnamon
$\frac{1}{4}$ teaspoon nutmeg	$\frac{1}{4}$ teaspoon nutmeg	$\frac{1}{4}$ teaspoon nutmeg
4 oz. blanched almonds	100 g. blanched almonds	1 cup blanched almonds
4 oz. candied peel	100 g. candied peel	$\frac{3}{4}$ cup candied peel
grated rind of 1 lemon	grated rind of 1 lemon	grated rind of 1 lemon
4 tablespoons brandy	4 tablespoons brandy	$\frac{1}{3}$ cup brandy
$1\frac{1}{4}$ lb. self-raising flour	500 g. self-raising flour	5 cups all-purpose flour sifted with 5 teaspoons baking powder
water icing	water icing	water icing

Put the honey and butter into a saucepan and heat until the butter is melted. Mix together the sugar, spices, shredded almonds, chopped peel and lemon rind. Pour onto the honey and butter and stir well together. Add the brandy and then work in the flour gradually, beating to a thick creamy batter. Put into a greased and lined 8- by 12-inch (20- by 30-cm.) tin and leave to stand in a cool place for 2 hours for the mixture to settle. Bake at the bottom of the oven for 1 hour. Cool, cut into small squares and ice with a thin glacé icing (see page 69) flavoured with a little brandy.

YEAST CAKES, BUNS AND TEACAKES

Cakes and buns made with yeast can easily be fitted into normal baking hours, and they are rewarding to make. Dried yeast may be substituted for fresh yeast in these recipes by using half the amount specified for fresh yeast.

A water and sugar syrup (1 tablespoon water to 2 tablespoons sugar) painted on after baking gives loaves and buns a sweet sticky finish. Remember when shaping buns that they swell up so should be made small rather than large. If you want to make a plait, divide the dough into 3, 5 or 7 equal portions and roll each between the fingers until they are long thin strands, then plait loosely rather than tightly. A bun twist can be simply made by rolling out the dough into a long sausage and tying the ends loosely together as if tying a knot. A Viennese twist is made with a tapering strand of dough about 2 ft. long as thick as your fist at one end and very thin at the other. Roll it up into a coil, starting from the thick end, and finally twist the end over the top to make a nice oval.

A cinnamon ring can be made with sweet yeast dough which has been rolled into a long rectangle and sprinkled with sugar and cinnamon. You then roll it up from the long side like a Swiss roll and form the roll into a circle. Snip two-thirds of the way through the dough at 1-inch intervals with a pair of scissors before baking.

Danish pastries

Cooking time: 30 minutes

Temperature: 375°F., 190°C., Gas Mark 5

Imperial	Metric	American
8 oz. plain flour	225 g. plain flour	2 cups all-purpose flour
½ teaspoon salt	½ teaspoon salt	½ teaspoon salt
2½ oz. sugar	65 g. sugar	5 tablespoons sugar
½ oz. fresh yeast	15 g. fresh yeast	½ oz. compressed yeast
¼ pint warm water	1½ dl. warm water	⅔ cup warm water
3 oz. butter	75 g. butter	6 tablespoons butter

Put the flour and salt in a warm basin. Cream the yeast with a little of the sugar and put into the flour together with the remaining sugar and the water. Mix to a soft, slightly sticky dough, and leave to rise in a warm place until increased by one-third in volume. Form the butter into a rectangle and dust with flour. Flatten the dough with the hands and fold with the butter in the centre like a parcel. Roll and fold twice like puff pastry. Leave in a cold place for 20 minutes, then roll and fold twice more and leave for 20 minutes. Roll out to ¼ inch (½ cm.) thick and form into one or more of the following shapes. Fold squares of pastry over fillings of dried fruit, jam, chopped nuts, marzipan or lemon curd to make envelope shapes. Crescents can be formed by rolling up triangles of pastry and curving the ends. Combs are made by folding a rectangle of dough lengthwise into three, cutting off 4-inch (10-cm.) pieces and slashing each one 5 times on one side so that the 'comb' opens out. Brush the pastries with melted butter, milk and egg mixed together, and bake without proving for 30 minutes. Dust with icing sugar, or cover with thin glacé icing (see page 69).

Fruit bannock (page 24), baps (page 78), Gloucester lardy cake (page 53), and yeast doughnuts (page 33)

Fruit bannock

Cooking time: 20 minutes

Temperature: 400°F., 200°C., Gas Mark 6

Illustrated on page 23

Imperial	Metric	American
Batter ingredients:	**Batter ingredients:**	**Batter ingredients:**
2 oz. plain flour	50 g. plain flour	$\frac{1}{2}$ cup all-purpose flour
1 oz. butter or white vegetable cooking fat, melted	25 g. butter or white vegetable cooking fat, melted	2 tablespoons melted butter or shortening
4 tablespoons warm milk	4 tablespoons warm milk	$\frac{1}{3}$ cup warm milk
$\frac{1}{4}$ oz. fresh yeast	10 g. fresh yeast	$\frac{1}{4}$ oz. compressed yeast
Additional ingredients:	**Additional ingredients:**	**Additional ingredients:**
6 oz. plain flour	175 g. plain flour	$1\frac{1}{2}$ cups all-purpose flour
1 oz. castor sugar	25 g. castor sugar	2 tablespoons granulated sugar
4 tablespoons warm milk	4 tablespoons warm milk	$\frac{1}{3}$ cup warm milk
1 oz. sultanas	25 g. sultanas	3 tablespoons white raisins
1 oz. currants	25 g. currants	3 tablespoons currants
$\frac{1}{2}$ oz. chopped candied peel	15 g. chopped candied peel	$1\frac{1}{2}$ tablespoons chopped candied peel

Blend the batter ingredients together in a mixing bowl and leave for 20 to 30 minutes until the batter is frothy. Add the additional ingredients and mix well. Knead the dough thoroughly for about 10 minutes on a lightly floured board. Put the dough to rise in a warm place under a damp cloth and leave for 1 hour, or until the dough springs back when pressed gently with a floured finger. Knead the dough again and shape into a ball. Flatten with the hands to approximately 8 inches (20 cm.) across and $\frac{1}{2}$ inch (just over 1 cm.) thick. Put on a greased and floured baking sheet and slash with a sharp knife into eight wedges. Brush top with milk, cover with a greased paper and leave to rise until the dough feels springy (about 45 minutes). Brush top again with milk, and bake towards the top of the oven for 20 minutes. Cool on a wire tray.

Lincolnshire plum bread

Cooking time: $2\frac{1}{2}$ hours

Temperature: 325°F., 170°C., Gas Mark 3

Imperial	Metric	American
12 oz. plain flour	350 g. plain flour	3 cups all-purpose flour
1 teaspoon baking powder	1 teaspoon baking powder	1 teaspoon baking powder
$\frac{1}{4}$ teaspoon nutmeg	$\frac{1}{4}$ teaspoon nutmeg	$\frac{1}{4}$ teaspoon nutmeg
pinch salt	pinch salt	pinch salt
4 oz. butter	100 g. butter	$\frac{1}{2}$ cup butter
6 oz. castor sugar	175 g. castor sugar	$\frac{3}{4}$ cup granulated sugar
6 oz. currants	175 g. currants	1 cup currants
3 oz. sultanas	75 g. sultanas	$\frac{1}{2}$ cup white raisins
3 oz. raisins	75 g. raisins	$\frac{1}{2}$ cup dark raisins
2 oz. chopped candied peel	50 g. chopped candied peel	$\frac{1}{3}$ cup chopped candied peel
2 oz. glacé cherries, chopped	50 g. glacé cherries, chopped	$\frac{1}{4}$ cup chopped candied cherries
1 oz. fresh yeast	25 g. fresh yeast	1 oz. compressed yeast
$\frac{1}{2}$ pint warm milk	3 dl. warm milk	$1\frac{1}{4}$ cups warm milk

Sieve the flour, baking powder, nutmeg and salt into a basin. Rub in the butter. Add most of the sugar, keeping a little back, and add the dried fruit. Cream the yeast with the remaining sugar, make a well in the dry ingredients, and add the yeast and warm milk, mixing well together. Turn the mixture into a greased large loaf tin and bake for $2\frac{1}{2}$ hours, covering with thick brown paper after $1\frac{1}{2}$ hours. Turn out on a wire rack to cool. Slice and spread with butter.

Chelsea buns

Cooking time: 15 minutes

Temperature: 450°F., 230°C., Gas Mark 8

Imperial	Metric	American
12 oz. plain flour	350 g. plain flour	3 cups all-purpose flour
3 oz. butter, melted	75 g. butter, melted	6 tablespoons melted butter
½ oz. fresh yeast	15 g. fresh yeast	½ oz. compressed yeast
12 tablespoons warm milk	scant ¼ litre warm milk	scant 1 cup warm milk
2 oz. castor sugar	50 g. castor sugar	⅓ cup granulated sugar
2 oz. currants	50 g. currants	⅓ cup currants

Put the flour in a warm basin, and add two-thirds of the butter. Cream the yeast with a pinch of sugar and add to the flour mixture with the milk. Knead well and leave to rise until double in size. Knead again and roll out to a square. Brush with the remaining melted butter and sprinkle with the sugar and currants. Roll up like a Swiss roll, and cut into slices 1½ inches (4 cm.) thick. Place cut side up on greased baking sheet, leaving room to swell. Leave to prove for 10 minutes. Brush with egg and bake for 15 minutes.

Iced plait

Cooking time: 15 minutes

Temperature: 450°F., 230°C., Gas Mark 8

Imperial	Metric	American
8 oz. plain flour	225 g. plain flour	2 cups all-purpose flour
pinch salt	pinch salt	pinch salt
½ oz. fresh yeast	15 g. fresh yeast	½ oz. compressed yeast
2 oz. sugar	50 g. sugar	¼ cup sugar
1 oz. butter	25 g. butter	2 tablespoons butter
6 tablespoons warm milk	6 tablespoons warm milk	½ cup warm milk
1 egg	1 egg	1 egg
3 oz. mixed dried fruit	75 g. mixed dried fruit	½ cup mixed dried fruit
chopped nuts and cherries	chopped nuts and cherries	chopped nuts and cherries

Put the flour and salt into a warm bowl. Cream the yeast with a little sugar, and add to the flour, together with the sugar, butter, warm milk, egg and dried fruit. Mix well, knead thoroughly, and leave in a warm place until double in size. Knead again, form into a long roll, divide in three and plait together, pressing the ends together firmly. Prove for 15 minutes, then brush with egg and bake for 15 minutes. When cold, coat with glacé icing (see page 69) and sprinkle thickly with chopped nuts and glacé cherries.

Apple cake

Cooking time: 20 minutes

Temperature: 425°F., 220°C., Gas Mark 7

Imperial	Metric	American
1 oz. fresh yeast	15 g. fresh yeast	1 oz. compressed yeast
4 tablespoons warm milk	4 tablespoons warm milk	⅓ cup warm milk
8 oz. plain flour	225 g. plain flour	2 cups all-purpose flour
1 oz. butter	25 g. butter	2 tablespoons butter
zest of 1 lemon	zest of 1 lemon	zest of 1 lemon
1 oz. sugar	25 g. sugar	2 tablespoons sugar
pinch salt	pinch salt	pinch salt
1 egg	1 egg	1 egg
apples	apples	apples

Dissolve the yeast in the warm milk. Mix in a little of the flour to make a thin paste, and leave to stand in a warm place for 30 minutes. Add the rest of the flour, the cool melted butter, the lemon zest, sugar and salt, and the beaten egg. Knead until smooth, cover with a cloth and leave to rise for 1½ hours. Divide between two 7-inch (18-cm.) sandwich cake tins. Dredge with sugar. Peel apples as required (or use halved plums, prunes or apricots), slice them thinly and arrange in overlapping slices to cover the cake. Sprinkle with cinnamon and castor sugar and bake for 20 minutes.

Streusel

Cooking time: 30 minutes

Temperature: 400°F., 200°C., Gas Mark 6

Imperial	Metric	American
1 oz. fresh yeast	25 g. fresh yeast	1 oz. compressed yeast
4 tablespoons warm milk	4 tablespoons warm milk	$\frac{1}{3}$ cup warm milk
2 tablespoons sugar	2 tablespoons sugar	3 tablespoons sugar
large pinch salt	large pinch salt	large pinch salt
2 eggs	2 eggs	2 eggs
zest of 1 lemon	zest of 1 lemon	zest of 1 lemon
4 oz. butter, melted	100 g. butter, melted	$\frac{1}{2}$ cup melted butter
8 oz. plain flour	225 g. plain flour	2 cups all-purpose flour

Topping:	**Topping:**	**Topping:**
1 oz. butter	25 g. butter	2 tablespoons butter
1 oz. flour	25 g. flour	$\frac{1}{4}$ cup flour
6 oz. sugar	175 g. sugar	$\frac{3}{4}$ cup sugar
2 oz. raisins	50 g. raisins	$\frac{1}{3}$ cup raisins
1 tablespoon cinnamon	1 tablespoon cinnamon	1 tablespoon cinnamon
melted butter	melted butter	melted butter

Dissolve the yeast in the lukewarm milk, stir in the sugar and salt and leave to stand for a few minutes. Beat in the eggs, the lemon zest and butter, and gradually work in the flour until the dough is soft and elastic. Cover with a cloth and leave in a warm place to rise for $1\frac{1}{2}$ hours. Divide the dough between two sandwich tins and prove again for 30 minutes. Rub the butter into the flour for the topping and mix with the sugar, raisins and cinnamon. Brush the cake with melted butter and sprinkle on the crumbled topping. Bake for 30 minutes.

Gugelhopf

Cooking time: 40 minutes

Temperature: 350°F., 180°C., Gas Mark 4

Imperial	Metric	American
1 oz. fresh yeast	25 g. fresh yeast	1 oz. compressed yeast
4 tablespoons warm milk	4 tablespoons warm milk	$\frac{1}{3}$ cup warm milk
8 oz. plain flour	225 g. plain flour	2 cups all-purpose flour
2 oz. butter, melted	50 g. butter, melted	$\frac{1}{4}$ cup melted butter
2 oz. sugar	50 g. sugar	$\frac{1}{4}$ cup sugar
2 eggs	2 eggs	2 eggs
zest and juice of 1 orange	zest and juice of 1 orange	zest and juice of 1 orange
2 oz. seedless raisins soaked in water	50 g. seedless raisins soaked in water	$\frac{1}{3}$ cup seedless raisins soaked in water

Dissolve the yeast in warm milk, mix in a little flour to make a thin paste and leave to rise in a warm place for 30 minutes. Beat thoroughly, adding butter, sugar, eggs, orange juice and zest and raisins. Beat in the remaining flour to make a slack dough. Grease a fluted ring mould thoroughly, and dust it with fine breadcrumbs or semolina. Fill it half full with the dough and leave to rise for about an hour until the dough reaches the top of the mould. Bake for 40 minutes. Cool and dust with icing sugar. There are dozens of Gugelhopf recipes, and almost any yeast cake baked in a fluted ring mould qualifies for the name. A pretty decoration is to arrange half blanched almonds in the flutes of the tin before the dough is poured in.

Chocolate brownies (page 39), florentines (page 48), and chocolate truffle cake (page 40)

SCONES AND GRIDDLECAKES

Scones are a kind of primitive bread, traditionally made from flour with buttermilk or sour milk, and baked on a hot 'scone' or bakestone. Many regional recipes are still cooked in this way, with the modern electric hotplate or top of a solid fuel cooker substituting for the bakestone. Another useful alternative for top-of-the-stove scone cooking is a heavy, flat-bottomed frying pan, though traditional heavy iron griddles can still be obtained.

   Scones should be baked 30 minutes before they are needed, being split and buttered when barely cool. Leftover scones can be stored in a plastic bag in the bread bin, toasting them if they get stale.

   For busy cooks, a basic dry scone mix is useful which can be stored in a cool place for several days to be made up in batches.

Apple griddlecakes

Cooking time: few minutes

Imperial	Metric	American
6 oz. plain flour	175 g. plain flour	1½ cups all-purpose flour
1¼ teaspoons baking powder	1¼ teaspoons baking powder	1¼ teaspoons baking powder
¾ teaspoon salt	¾ teaspoon salt	¾ teaspoon salt
3 tablespoons sugar	3 tablespoons sugar	¼ cup sugar
1 egg	1 egg	1 egg
⅓ pint milk	2 dl. milk	¾ cup milk
3 tablespoons melted butter	3 tablespoons melted butter	¼ cup melted butter
1 large hard sweet apple	1 large hard sweet apple	1 large hard sweet apple

Sift the flour into a basin with the baking powder and salt. Stir in the sugar, then add the egg, milk and butter to make a creamy batter. Peel the apple and cut in very thin slices, then add to batter. Heat a greased griddle or frying pan, and drop the mixture on in spoonfuls. Cook until golden on both sides. Serve sprinkled with castor sugar.

Drop scones

Cooking time: few minutes

Imperial	Metric	American
8 oz. plain flour	225 g. plain flour	3 cups plain flour
¼ teaspoon salt	¼ teaspoon salt	¼ teaspoon salt
½ teaspoon bicarbonate of soda	½ teaspoon bicarbonate of soda	½ teaspoon baking soda
1 teaspoon cream of tartar	1 teaspoon cream of tartar	1 teaspoon cream of tartar
1 tablespoon sugar	1 tablespoon sugar	1 tablespoon sugar
1 egg	1 egg	1 egg
¼ pint milk	1½ dl. milk	⅔ cup milk

Sieve together the flour, salt, soda and cream of tartar. Stir in the sugar, and mix to a thick batter with the egg and milk. Lightly grease a hot griddle or thick frying pan and drop the mixture on in spoonfuls. When bubbles appear on the surface, turn quickly and cook the other side. Serve wrapped in a clean cloth to keep scones warm and soft.

Basic dry scone mix

Cooking time: 12 minutes

Temperature: 450°F., 230°C., Gas Mark 8

Imperial	Metric	American
1 lb. self-raising flour	450 g. self-raising flour	4 cups all-purpose flour
2 teaspoons baking powder	2 teaspoons baking powder	6 teaspoons baking powder
3 oz. butter	75 g. butter	6 tablespoons butter

Sift together the flour and baking powder, and rub in the butter until the mixture looks like fine breadcrumbs. Store in a plastic container in a cold place, keeping tightly covered. Half this mixture with the addition of $\frac{1}{4}$ pint ($1\frac{1}{2}$ decilitres, $\frac{2}{3}$ cup) milk or water will make 12 scones. When the scones are mixed, roll out and cut in rounds. Place close together on a greased baking sheet and bake for 12 minutes.

Note: If you prefer to use plain flour, use one teaspoon bicarbonate of soda and 2 teaspoons cream of tartar as raising agents. If you use sour milk to mix, which gives a better texture, use only 1 teaspoon cream of tartar.

Variations

Sweet scones: Use milk, or substitute an egg for 3 tablespoons of the milk.
Cheese scones: Add 4 oz. finely grated dry cheese, and use water for a fluffy texture. This dough can also be cooked in 2 1-lb. loaf tins at 375°F., 190°C., Gas Mark 5 for 40–45 minutes.

Potato cakes

Cooking time: few minutes

Imperial	Metric	American
8 oz. cold mashed potato	225 g. cold mashed potato	1 cup cold mashed potato
1 oz. butter	25 g. butter	2 tablespoons butter
2 oz. plain flour	50 g. plain flour	$\frac{1}{2}$ cup all-purpose flour
pinch salt	pinch salt	pinch salt
4 tablespoons milk	4 tablespoons milk	$\frac{1}{3}$ cup milk

Mash or sieve the potatoes, work in the butter and add the flour and salt, working the mixture until the flour is well blended into the potatoes. Blend to a stiff dough with the milk. Roll out lightly on a floured board and cut into rounds or squares. Cook on a lightly greased hot griddle until golden brown on both sides. Split and butter and serve while hot.

Wheatmeal spoon scones

Cooking time: 15 minutes

Temperature: 450°F., 230°C., Gas Mark 8

Imperial	Metric	American
10 oz. wholemeal flour	275 g. wholemeal flour	$2\frac{1}{2}$ cups whole-wheat flour
6 oz. plain flour	175 g. plain flour	$1\frac{1}{2}$ cups all-purpose flour
1 teaspoon salt	1 teaspoon salt	1 teaspoon salt
1 teaspoon bicarbonate of soda	1 teaspoon bicarbonate of soda	1 teaspoon baking soda
2 teaspoons cream of tartar	2 teaspoons cream of tartar	2 teaspoons cream of tartar
2 oz. granulated sugar	50 g. granulated sugar	$\frac{1}{4}$ cup granulated sugar
2 oz. butter	50 g. butter	$\frac{1}{4}$ cup butter
1 tablespoon black treacle	1 tablespoon black treacle	1 tablespoon molasses
scant $\frac{1}{2}$ pint milk	$\frac{1}{4}$ litre milk	1 cup milk

Sieve together dry ingredients and stir in the sugar. Rub in the butter, then mix in the treacle and milk to give a heavy dropping consistency. Drop spoonfuls of the mixture on to a baking sheet dusted with wholemeal flour. Brush lightly with milk and dredge with flour or rolled oats. Bake for 15 minutes.

Tyneside singin' hinny

Cooking time: several minutes

Imperial	Metric	American
8 oz. plain flour	225 g. plain flour	2 cups all-purpose flour
$\frac{1}{2}$ teaspoon baking powder	$\frac{1}{2}$ teaspoon baking powder	$\frac{1}{2}$ teaspoon baking powder
$\frac{1}{2}$ teaspoon salt	$\frac{1}{2}$ teaspoon salt	$\frac{1}{2}$ teaspoon salt
2 oz. butter	50 g. butter	$\frac{1}{4}$ cup butter
2 oz. lard	50 g. lard	$\frac{1}{4}$ cup lard
3 oz. currants	75 g. currants	$\frac{1}{2}$ cup currants
milk	milk	milk

Sift the flour, baking powder and salt together and rub in the fats until the mixture is like fine breadcrumbs. Add the currants and mix with enough milk to make a stiff paste. Roll out into a large cake $\frac{1}{2}$ inch (1 cm.) thick (or cut into 3-inch (8-cm.) rounds), prick top and put on a greased griddle or frying pan. Cook both sides until golden; split and butter to serve.

Walnut and honey scones

Cooking time: 10 minutes

Temperature: 425°F., 220°C., Gas Mark 7

Illustrated on page 31

Imperial	Metric	American
1 lb. self-raising flour	450 g. self-raising flour	4 cups all-purpose flour sifted with $4\frac{1}{4}$ teaspoons baking powder
1 teaspoon salt	1 teaspoon salt	1 teaspoon salt
4 oz. butter	100 g. butter	$\frac{1}{2}$ cup butter
2 tablespoons castor sugar	2 tablespoons castor sugar	$2\frac{1}{2}$ tablespoons granulated sugar
2 oz. walnuts, finely chopped	50 g. walnuts, finely chopped	$\frac{1}{2}$ cup finely chopped walnuts
2 tablespoons clear honey	2 tablespoons clear honey	$2\frac{1}{2}$ tablespoons clear honey
generous $\frac{1}{4}$ pint cold milk	2 dl. cold milk	$\frac{3}{4}$ cup cold milk

Sift the flour and salt into a basin and rub in the butter. Add the sugar and walnuts and mix to a soft but not sticky dough with the honey and milk. Turn on to a lightly floured board, knead quickly and roll out to $\frac{1}{2}$ inch (1 cm.) thickness. Cut into rounds and put on a greased baking sheet. Brush tops with beaten egg or milk and bake for 10 minutes.

Cottage cheese griddlecakes

Cooking time: few minutes

Imperial	Metric	American
1 tablespoon melted butter	1 tablespoon melted butter	1 tablespoon melted butter
4 oz. cottage cheese	100 g. cottage cheese	$\frac{1}{2}$ cup cottage cheese
2 eggs	2 eggs	2 eggs
2 oz. self-raising flour	50 g. self-raising flour	$\frac{1}{2}$ cup all-purpose flour sifted with $\frac{1}{2}$ teaspoon baking powder
1 tablespoon milk	1 tablespoon milk	1 tablespoon milk

Mix the butter with the cottage cheese and gradually whisk in the eggs. Stir in the flour and milk and mix to a smooth thick batter. Drop spoonfuls on to a hot greased griddle or frying pan and turn several times. Serve freshly cooked with crisp hot bacon, honey, jam or jelly. These scones are very light and digestible, and particularly good for those who do not want much starch in their diet.

Honey and walnut cheesecake (page 37), and walnut and honey scones

Derbyshire oatcake

Cooking time: several minutes

Imperial	Metric	American
8 oz. fine or medium oatmeal	225 g. fine or medium oatmeal	1⅓ cups ground oatmeal
8 oz. plain flour	225 g. plain flour	2 cups all-purpose flour
pinch salt	pinch salt	pinch salt
1 oz. fresh yeast	25 g. fresh yeast	1 oz. fresh yeast
1 teaspoon sugar	1 teaspoon sugar	1 teaspoon sugar
1¼ pint lukewarm water	7½ dl. lukewarm water	generous 3 cups lukewarm water

Sift together the oatmeal, flour and salt. Cream the yeast and sugar and add the warm water. Stir into the dry ingredients and leave in a warm place for 30 minutes. Heat griddle and grease lightly. Pour on a little batter at a time and cook about 2 minutes. Turn and cook the other side. Serve hot with butter or dripping, or with crisp hot bacon.
Note: Fresh yeast may be replaced by half the quantity of dried yeast.

Caerphilly scones

Cooking time: 15 minutes

Temperature: 450°F., 230°C., Gas Mark 8

Imperial	Metric	American
12 oz. plain flour	350 g. plain flour	3 cups all-purpose flour
3 teaspoons baking powder	3 teaspoons baking powder	3 teaspoons baking powder
¼ teaspoon salt	¼ teaspoon salt	¼ teaspoon salt
3 oz. Caerphilly cheese, grated	75 g. Caerphilly cheese, grated	¾ cup grated Caerphilly or other mild cheese
2 oz. Parmesan cheese, grated	50 g. Parmesan cheese, grated	½ cup grated Parmesan cheese
pinch pepper	pinch pepper	pinch pepper
1½ oz. butter	65 g. butter	3 tablespoons butter
½ pint milk	3 dl. milk	1¼ cups milk

Sift together the flour, baking powder and salt. Add the grated cheeses and the pepper. Rub in the butter and mix in the milk to make a soft dough. Roll out ½ inch (1 cm.) thick, cut into rounds and put on greased baking sheet. Bake for 15 minutes. Serve hot with butter.

Irish griddle bread

Cooking time: 20 minutes

Imperial	Metric	American
8 oz. wholemeal flour	225 g. wholemeal flour	2 cups whole-wheat flour
8 oz. plain flour	225 g. plain flour	2 cups all-purpose flour
2 teaspoons sugar	2 teaspoons sugar	2 teaspoons sugar
1 teaspoon bicarbonate of soda	1 teaspoon bicarbonate of soda	1 teaspoon baking soda
1 teaspoon salt	1 teaspoon salt	1 teaspoon salt
2 teaspoons dripping	2 teaspoons dripping	2 teaspoons meat drippings
milk	milk	milk

Mix together the flours, and add the sugar, soda and salt. Rub in the dripping and mix in enough milk to make a dough which is stiff but will roll easily. Roll out in a round 1 inch (2½ cm.) thick, and cut into four sections. Cook on a hot griddle for 10 minutes each side.

DOUGHNUTS AND FRIED CAKES

The doughnut is the most popular type of fried cake and may be made with yeast or baking powder as a raising agent. As a change from the somewhat heavy doughnut, crullers are light and crisp and very good with coffee.

To fry cakes, lard or vegetable fat should be heated to 370°F. (190°C.). If a thermometer is not available, the fat is at the correct temperature when a 1-inch ($2\frac{1}{2}$-cm.) cube of bread turns golden brown in 60 seconds. Be sure to fry only small quantities at a time to avoid cooling the fat unnecessarily. Doughnuts and fried cakes normally require 3 to 5 minutes, and should be cooked in a basket for easy draining. As soon as they are cooked, they should be placed on absorbent paper to blot up surplus fat. Be careful not to pierce a fried cake when lifting it from the fat or it will become soggy and greasy. Cool the doughnuts before rolling them in sugar; this is easily done by shaking 2 or 3 doughnuts in a paper bag with sugar until well coated.

Baking powder doughnuts

Cooking time: 3–5 minutes

Imperial	Metric	American
6 oz. plain flour	175 g. plain flour	$1\frac{1}{2}$ cups all-purpose flour
$\frac{1}{2}$ teaspoon salt	$\frac{1}{2}$ teaspoon salt	$\frac{1}{2}$ teaspoon salt
1 teaspoon baking powder	1 teaspoon baking powder	1 teaspoon baking powder
2 oz. margarine	50 g. margarine	$\frac{1}{4}$ cup margarine
1 oz. sugar	25 g. sugar	2 tablespoons sugar
1 egg	1 egg	1 egg
milk	milk	milk
raspberry jam	raspberry jam	raspberry jam

Sieve the flour, salt and baking powder, and rub in the margarine. Add the sugar and mix to a light dough with the beaten egg and a little milk. Turn on to a floured board and roll out to $\frac{1}{4}$-inch ($\frac{1}{2}$-cm.) thickness. Cut into small rounds, put a little raspberry jam in the centre of each, and put two together like a sandwich, pinching round the edges to secure. Fry in hot fat, turning when brown on the underside. Toss in sugar, or sugar and cinnamon.

Yeast doughnuts

Cooking time: 3–5 minutes

Illustrated on page 23

Imperial	Metric	American
8 oz. plain flour	225 g. plain flour	2 cups all-purpose flour
2 teaspoons sugar	2 teaspoons sugar	2 teaspoons sugar
$\frac{1}{2}$ oz. fresh yeast	15 g. fresh yeast	$\frac{1}{2}$ oz. compressed yeast
$\frac{1}{4}$ pint lukewarm milk or water	$1\frac{1}{2}$ dl. lukewarm milk or water	$\frac{2}{3}$ cup lukewarm milk or water
1 teaspoon salt	1 teaspoon salt	1 teaspoon salt
$\frac{1}{2}$ oz. margarine	15 g. margarine	1 tablespoon margarine
raspberry jam	raspberry jam	raspberry jam

Sieve the flour and mix in the sugar. Whisk the yeast in half the milk; add the salt and melted margarine to the remaining milk, and cool to luke-warm. Add both liquids to the flour, mix and knead well, and prove for 1 hour. Knead lightly, cut into 16 pieces, and form into balls. Flatten the balls, put jam in the centre, and fold edges to enclose the jam, pressing together firmly. Prove for 20 minutes, then fry in hot fat, drain and cool.

Spiced doughnut rings

Cooking time: 3–5 minutes

Imperial	Metric	American
8 oz. self-raising flour	225 g. self-raising flour	2 cups all-purpose flour sifted with 2 teaspoons baking powder
$\frac{1}{2}$ teaspoon salt	$\frac{1}{2}$ teaspoon salt	$\frac{1}{2}$ teaspoon salt
$\frac{1}{4}$ teaspoon cinnamon	$\frac{1}{4}$ teaspoon cinnamon	$\frac{1}{4}$ teaspoon cinnamon
$\frac{1}{4}$ teaspoon nutmeg	$\frac{1}{4}$ teaspoon nutmeg	$\frac{1}{4}$ teaspoon nutmeg
$\frac{1}{2}$ oz. cooking fat	15 g. cooking fat	1 tablespoon shortening
2 oz. castor sugar	50 g. castor sugar	$\frac{1}{4}$ cup granulated sugar
1 egg	1 egg	1 egg
4 tablespoons milk	4 tablespoons milk	$\frac{1}{3}$ cup milk
cinnamon and sugar	cinnamon and sugar	cinnamon and sugar

Sieve the flour, salt and spices into a basin and rub in the cooking fat. Add the sugar and mix in the egg and milk to make a fairly soft dough. Roll out $\frac{1}{4}$ inch ($\frac{1}{2}$ cm.) thick on a floured board and cut into 3-inch (8-cm.) rounds. Cut out centres with $1\frac{1}{2}$-inch (4-cm.) cutter. Fry in hot fat until golden, drain well and toss in a mixture of cinnamon and sugar.

Afternoon tea doughnuts

Cooking time: 3–5 minutes

Imperial	Metric	American
1 egg	1 egg	1 egg
2 tablespoons sugar	2 tablespoons sugar	$2\frac{1}{2}$ tablespoons sugar
$\frac{1}{2}$ teaspoon salt	$\frac{1}{2}$ teaspoon salt	$\frac{1}{2}$ teaspoon salt
3 tablespoons milk	3 tablespoons milk	$\frac{1}{4}$ cup milk
1 tablespoon melted fat	1 tablespoon melted fat	1 tablespoon melted shortening
4 oz. plain flour	100 g. plain flour	1 cup all-purpose flour
2 teaspoons baking powder	2 teaspoons baking powder	2 teaspoons baking powder

Beat the egg until light and add the sugar, salt, milk and fat. Sift the flour with the baking powder and stir in. Pipe the batter through a pastry tube in finger lengths. Fry in hot deep fat until golden.

Variation

Sour milk doughnuts: Substitute sour milk for fresh, and use 1 teaspoon soda and 1 teaspoon baking powder as a raising agent.

Chocolate doughnuts: Add $1\frac{1}{2}$ oz. (40 g.) melted plain chocolate, a pinch of cinnamon and 1 teaspoon vanilla to the basic mixture.

Lemon doughnuts: Flavour with 2 tablespoons lemon juice, 1 teaspoon lemon rind, and a pinch of nutmeg.

Christmas crullers

Cooking time: 3–5 minutes

Imperial	Metric	American
4 egg yolks	4 egg yolks	4 egg yolks
1 oz. icing sugar	25 g. icing sugar	$\frac{1}{4}$ cup confectioners' sugar
3 tablespoons butter	3 tablespoons butter	$\frac{1}{4}$ cup butter
6 oz. plain flour	175 g. plain flour	$1\frac{1}{2}$ cups all-purpose flour
1 tablespoon brandy	1 tablespoon brandy	1 tablespoon brandy
1 tablespoon grated lemon rind	1 tablespoon grated lemon rind	1 tablespoon grated lemon rind

Mix all the ingredients together and stir until well blended. Chill the mixture, then roll out $\frac{1}{4}$ inch ($\frac{1}{2}$ cm.) thick. With a pastry wheel, cut strips 3 inches (8 cm.) long and $\frac{3}{4}$ inch (2 cm.) wide. Cut a gash lengthwise through the centre of each strip and twist end through so each strip looks like a knot. Fry until light brown and drain on paper. Serve plain, or with jam.

CHEESECAKES

Cheesecakes form a halfway mark between cakes and puddings, and vary widely in ingredients and appearance. They may be baked in tins lined with biscuit crumbs or pastry, or they can simply be set in the refrigerator. They may be plain, or flavoured with orange, lemon or spices, or enhanced with the addition of fruit or nuts.

Cream cheese can often be used, but cottage cheese is recommended because it is inexpensive and easily digested. The main essential of a good cheesecake is that the basic cheese mixture should be smooth and on the dry side, so the cottage cheese should be sieved. Chilled unbaked cheesecakes keep their shape well, but the baked varieties tend to fall in the middle, particularly when the egg whites are whisked separately before addition.

To make these cakes most successfully, a spring-sided cake tin is best, or a tin with a removable base.

Lemon cheesecake

Imperial	Metric	American
2 eggs	2 eggs	2 eggs
2 oz. castor sugar	50 g. castor sugar	$\frac{1}{4}$ cup granulated sugar
3 tablespoons lemon juice	3 tablespoons lemon juice	$\frac{1}{4}$ cup lemon juice
3 tablespoons orange juice	3 tablespoons orange juice	$\frac{1}{4}$ cup orange juice
1 tablespoon powdered gelatine	1 tablespoon powdered gelatine	1 tablespoon powdered gelatin
2 tablespoons cold water	2 tablespoons cold water	2 tablespoons cold water
12 oz. cottage cheese	350 g. cottage cheese	$1\frac{1}{2}$ cups cottage cheese
$\frac{1}{4}$ pint whipped cream	$1\frac{1}{2}$ dl. whipped cream	$\frac{2}{3}$ cup whipped cream
sweet biscuit crumbs	sweet biscuit crumbs	cookie crumbs

Separate the eggs. Beat the egg yolks with the sugar until pale and creamy. Add the fruit juices and stir the mixture in a bowl over boiling water until it begins to thicken and coat the spoon. Add the gelatine softened in the cold water, and stir until dissolved. Cool, then stir in sieved cottage cheese and whipped cream. Whisk the egg whites stiffly and fold into the mixture. Butter an 8-inch (20-cm.) deep round tin, and sprinkle thickly with sweet biscuit crumbs. Pour in the mixture and chill until firm. Turn out of the tin and pipe with whipped cream and decorate with crystallised lemon slices.

Almond cheesecake

Cooking time: 40 minutes

Temperature: 400°F., 200°C., Gas Mark 6

Imperial	Metric	American
2 oz. butter	50 g. butter	¼ cup butter
2 oz. castor sugar	50 g. castor sugar	¼ cup granulated sugar
grated rind of 1 lemon	grated rind of 1 lemon	grated rind of 1 lemon
3 egg yolks	3 egg yolks	3 egg yolks
1 lb. cottage cheese	450 g. cottage cheese	2 cups cottage cheese
2 oz. ground almonds	50 g. ground almonds	½ cup ground almonds
1 oz. sultanas	25 g. sultanas	3 tablespoons white raisins
2 oz. soft breadcrumbs	50 g. soft breadcrumbs	1 cup soft bread crumbs
pinch salt	pinch salt	pinch salt

Cream the butter, sugar and lemon rind. Beat in the egg yolks. Stir in the sieved cottage cheese, ground almonds, sultanas, breadcrumbs and salt. Put into a buttered 8-inch (20-cm.) round tin, and bake for 40 minutes. Leave to cool with the oven turned off. Sprinkle with sugar before serving.

Cheesecake torte

Cooking time: 1 hour

Temperature: 350°F., 180°C., Gas Mark 4

Imperial	Metric	American
¼ pint double cream	1½ dl. double cream	⅔ cup whipping cream
1 oz. cornflour	25 g. cornflour	¼ cup cornstarch
1 lb. cottage cheese	450 g. cottage cheese	2 cups cottage cheese
4 egg whites	4 egg whites	4 egg whites
6 oz. castor sugar	175 g. castor sugar	¾ cup granulated sugar
1 teaspoon vanilla essence	1 teaspoon vanilla essence	1 teaspoon vanilla extract
sweet biscuit crumbs	sweet biscuit crumbs	cookie crumbs

Whip the cream and blend with cornflour. Add the sieved cottage cheese. Whisk the egg whites until stiff and fold in the sugar and vanilla. Fold lightly into the cheese mixture. Sprinkle a buttered 8-inch (20-cm.) deep round tin with sweet biscuit crumbs and put in the cheese mixture. Bake for 1 hour. Serve straight from the oven topped with toasted almonds, fruit or cream, or serve cold with cream and fruit.

Old-fashioned cheesecake

Cooking time: 15–20 minutes

Temperature: 375°F., 190°C., Gas Mark 5

Imperial	Metric	American
8 oz. cottage cheese	225 g. cottage cheese	1 cup cottage cheese
6 oz. castor sugar	175 g. castor sugar	¾ cup granulated sugar
6 egg yolks	6 egg yolks	6 egg yolks
2 oz. butter	50 g. butter	¼ cup butter
finely grated rind of 2 lemons	finely grated rind of 2 lemons	finely grated rind of 2 lemons
pinch salt	pinch salt	pinch salt
pinch nutmeg	pinch nutmeg	pinch nutmeg
12 oz. puff pastry	350 g. puff pastry	puff pastry made with 3 cups flour
chopped candied peel	chopped candied peel	chopped candied peel
currants	currants	currants
sultanas	sultanas	white raisins

Blend together the sieved cottage cheese, sugar, egg yolks, butter, lemon rind, salt and nutmeg. Line 30 tartlet tins with the puff pastry and spoon the cheese mixture into the cases. Sprinkle with peel, currants and sultanas. Bake until the pastry is light and golden in colour.

Coventry tarts

Cooking time: 15–20 minutes

Temperature: 375°F., 190°C., Gas Mark 5

Imperial	Metric	American
8 oz. cottage cheese	225 g. cottage cheese	1 cup cottage cheese
4 oz. castor sugar	100 g. castor sugar	½ cup granulated sugar
pinch salt	pinch salt	pinch salt
pinch nutmeg	pinch nutmeg	pinch nutmeg
1 tablespoon orange or pineapple juice	1 tablespoon orange or pineapple juice	1 tablespoon orange or pineapple juice
4 oz. butter	100 g. butter	½ cup butter
1 egg	1 egg	1 egg
8 oz. shortcrust pastry	225 g. shortcrust pastry	plain pastry made with 2 cups flour
apple or currant jelly	apple or currant jelly	apple or currant jelly

Blend together the sieved cottage cheese, sugar, salt, nutmeg, fruit juice, butter and beaten egg. Line 24 tartlet tins with the shortcrust pastry and fill with the cheese mixture. Bake until the pastry is light and golden in colour. Top each tart with jelly before serving.

Honey cheesecakes

Cooking time: 30 minutes

Temperature: 400°F., 200°C., Gas Mark 6

Imperial	Metric	American
4 oz. cottage cheese	100 g. cottage cheese	½ cup cottage cheese
2 oz. honey	50 g. honey	3 tablespoons honey
2 oz. castor sugar	50 g. castor sugar	¼ cup granulated sugar
½ teaspoon cinnamon	½ teaspoon cinnamon	½ teaspoon cinnamon
2 beaten eggs	2 beaten eggs	2 beaten eggs
4 oz. shortcrust pastry	100 g. shortcrust pastry	plain pastry made with 1 cup flour
cinnamon	cinnamon	cinnamon
castor sugar	castor sugar	granulated sugar

Blend together the sieved cottage cheese, honey, sugar, cinnamon and eggs. Line a 7-inch (18-cm.) pie plate with short pastry and fill with the cheese mixture. Sprinkle thickly with a mixture of cinnamon and castor sugar and bake for 30 minutes.

Honey and walnut cheesecake

Cooking time: 40 minutes

Temperature: 425°F., 220°C., Gas Mark 7; then 375°F., 190°C., Gas Mark 5

Illustrated on page 31

Imperial	Metric	American
6 oz. shortcrust pastry	175 g. shortcrust pastry	plain pastry made with 1½ cups flour
3 tablespoons sultanas	3 tablespoons sultanas	¼ cup white raisins
1 tablespoon chopped candied peel	1 tablespoon chopped candied peel	1 tablespoon chopped candied peel
2 eggs	2 eggs	2 eggs
8 oz. cottage cheese	225 g. cottage cheese	1 cup cottage cheese
2 tablespoons double cream	2 tablespoons double cream	3 tablespoons whipping cream
1 tablespoon honey	1 tablespoon honey	1 tablespoon honey
2 teaspoons lemon juice	2 teaspoons lemon juice	2 teaspoons lemon juice
1 teaspoon cinnamon	1 teaspoon cinnamon	1 teaspoon cinnamon
1 oz. walnut kernels	25 g. walnut kernels	¼ cup walnut kernels

Line an 8-inch (20-cm.) pie plate with the pastry and sprinkle the bottom with the sultanas and peel. Separate the eggs. Blend the sieved cottage cheese with the cream, honey, egg yolks and lemon juice. Whisk the egg whites stiffly and fold into the cheese mixture. Put into the pastry case and sprinkle with cinnamon. Bake at 425°F. for 10 minutes, then reduce the heat to 375°F. and bake for 30 minutes. Sprinkle with finely chopped walnuts before serving.

CHOCOLATE CAKES

Chocolate cakes are always popular, whether in a simple form for an everyday family cake, or rich with cream, liqueurs and nuts for a tea or coffee party. They can even be eaten as a dessert after a simple main course.

The secret of a good moist chocolate cake is to use plain melted chocolate, either in block or chip form. If cocoa is used in the recipe, the cake is improved if the cocoa is cooked in a little liquid before adding it to the cake mixture. Orange and rum flavours blend well with chocolate, while a pinch of instant coffee or a few drops of coffee essence will give a mocha flavour and bring out the richness of the chocolate. Walnuts and hazelnuts are natural partners for chocolate, and make useful cake decorations. Grated plain chocolate is another finish for a simple iced chocolate cake.

If there is any cake left in the tin, it can be used as an excellent pudding. Fresh chocolate cake is delicious served with vanilla ice cream, or with chocolate sauce to which a little coffee or a dash of rum has been added. Another way to serve it is spread with apricot jam, topped with egg custard and well chilled before serving, spiked with toasted almonds. Chocolate cake layered with sweetened whipped cream can be frozen for eight hours, then served piped with fresh whipped cream. Another pudding can be made with a mixture of small pieces of broken chocolate cake, marshmallows, chopped nuts and candied peel folded into whipped cream chilled for three hours.

Simple chocolate cake

Cooking time: 35 minutes

Temperature: 350°F., 180°C., Gas Mark 4

Imperial	Metric	American
1 tablespoon cocoa	1 tablespoon cocoa	1 tablespoon cocoa powder
2 tablespoons milk	2 tablespoons milk	3 tablespoons milk
4 oz. butter	100 g. butter	$\frac{1}{2}$ cup butter
5 oz. castor sugar	125 g. castor sugar	$\frac{2}{3}$ cup granulated sugar
2 eggs	2 eggs	2 eggs
4 oz. self-raising flour	100 g. self-raising flour	1 cup all-purpose flour sifted with 1 teaspoon baking powder

Blend the cocoa with the milk and cook over gentle heat until smooth and thick. Leave until cold. Cream together the butter and sugar. Slowly beat in the eggs and chocolate mixture, and fold in the flour. Bake in an 8-inch (20-cm.) deep round tin for 35 minutes. When cool, top with icing and decorate.

French chocolate cake

Cooking time: 1 hour 10 minutes

Temperature: 350°F., 180°C.,
   Gas Mark 4

Imperial	Metric	American
4 oz. plain chocolate	100 g. plain chocolate	$\frac{2}{3}$ cup semi-sweet chocolate pieces
1 tablespoon water	1 tablespoon water	1 tablespoon water
4 oz. butter	100 g. butter	$\frac{1}{2}$ cup butter
5 oz. castor sugar	125 g. castor sugar	$\frac{2}{3}$ cup granulated sugar
2 oz. ground almonds	50 g. ground almonds	$\frac{1}{2}$ cup ground almonds
3 oz. coarse stale white breadcrumbs	75 g. coarse stale white breadcrumbs	$\frac{3}{4}$ cup coarse stale white bread crumbs
$\frac{1}{2}$ teaspoon vanilla essence	$\frac{1}{2}$ teaspoon vanilla essence	$\frac{1}{2}$ teaspoon vanilla extract
3 eggs	3 eggs	3 eggs
Icing:	**Icing:**	**Icing:**
2 oz. plain chocolate	50 g. plain chocolate	$\frac{1}{3}$ cup semi-sweet chocolate pieces
2 teaspoons sugar	2 teaspoons sugar	2 teaspoons sugar
1 tablespoon water	1 tablespoon water	1 tablespoon water
$\frac{1}{2}$ oz. butter	15 g. butter	1 tablespoon butter

Melt the chocolate in the water in a double saucepan over hot water. Cream the butter and sugar and add the melted chocolate, almonds, breadcrumbs and vanilla. Separate the eggs and add the yolks to the batter. Blend well together. Beat the egg whites stiffly and fold them gently into the chocolate mixture. Put into a greased and lined 7-inch (18-cm.) deep round tin standing in a pan of water. Bake until a skewer pushed into the centre of the cake comes out cleanly. Ice the cake while still warm by melting chocolate and sugar in the water and beating in the butter; cool the mixture slightly, then spread on the cake.

Chocolate brownies

Cooking time: 30 minutes

Temperature: 350°F., 180°C.,
   Gas Mark 4

Illustrated on page 27

Imperial	Metric	American
8 oz. granulated sugar	225 g. granulated sugar	1 cup granulated sugar
$1\frac{1}{2}$ oz. cocoa	40 g. cocoa	6 tablespoons cocoa powder
3 oz. self-raising flour	75 g. self-raising flour	$\frac{3}{4}$ cup all-purpose flour sifted with $\frac{3}{4}$ teaspoon baking powder
$\frac{1}{2}$ teaspoon salt	$\frac{1}{2}$ teaspoon salt	$\frac{1}{2}$ teaspoon salt
2 eggs	2 eggs	2 eggs
2 tablespoons creamy milk	2 tablespoons creamy milk	3 tablespoons creamy milk
4 oz. butter or margarine, melted	100 g. butter or margarine, melted	$\frac{1}{2}$ cup melted butter or margarine
3 oz. shelled walnuts or 3 oz. seedless raisins	75 g. shelled walnuts or 75 g. seedless raisins	$\frac{3}{4}$ cup shelled walnuts or $\frac{1}{2}$ cup seedless raisins
Quick icing:	**Quick icing:**	**Quick icing:**
4 oz. plain chocolate	100 g. plain chocolate	$\frac{2}{3}$ cup semi-sweet chocolate pieces

Stir together the sugar, cocoa, flour and salt. Beat the eggs and milk, and add to the dry mixture, together with the melted butter or margarine. Stir in the broken walnuts or raisins. Pour into an 8- by 12-inch (20- by 30-cm.) tin and bake for 30 minutes. Cool in the tin and cut in squares. For the icing, sprinkle the chopped plain chocolate on the cake while it is still hot, leave to melt for a few minutes, then spread with a palette knife.

Devil's food

Cooking time: 35 minutes

Temperature: 350°F., 180°C., Gas Mark 4

Imperial	Metric	American
4 oz. plain chocolate	100 g. plain chocolate	⅔ cup semi-sweet chocolate pieces
4 oz. soft brown sugar	100 g. soft brown sugar	½ cup soft brown sugar
⅓ pint milk	2 dl. milk	¾ cup milk
3 eggs	3 eggs	3 eggs
8 oz. granulated sugar	225 g. granulated sugar	1 cup granulated sugar
3 oz. butter	75 g. butter	6 tablespoons butter
10 oz. plain flour	275 g. plain flour	2½ cups all-purpose flour
¼ teaspoon salt	¼ teaspoon salt	¼ teaspoon salt
1 teaspoon bicarbonate of soda	1 teaspoon bicarbonate of soda	1 teaspoon baking soda
¼ pint milk	1½ dl. milk	⅔ cup milk

Melt the chocolate in top of a double saucepan, and add the brown sugar, ⅓ pint milk and 1 slightly beaten egg yolk. Stir and cook over hot water until smooth, then leave to cool. Beat the 3 egg whites until stiff, beat in half the granulated sugar and leave on one side. Cream the butter and remaining sugar, and add the remaining 2 well-beaten egg yolks. Mix and sift the flour, salt and bicarbonate of soda, and add to the butter mixture alternately with the ¼ pint milk. Add the chocolate mixture and beat well, and finally fold in the egg whites. Put into two buttered and floured 7-inch (18-cm.) square tins, and bake for 35 minutes. Fill and ice with a white or chocolate icing.

Chocolate truffle cake

Illustrated on page 27

Imperial	Metric	American
4 oz. butter	100 g. butter	½ cup butter
1 tablespoon sugar	1 tablespoon sugar	1 tablespoon sugar
2 tablespoons cocoa	2 tablespoons cocoa	2½ tablespoons cocoa powder
1 tablespoon golden syrup	1 tablespoon golden syrup	1 tablespoon corn syrup
8 oz. fine biscuit crumbs	225 g. fine biscuit crumbs	2 cups fine cookie crumbs
2 oz. milk chocolate	50 g. milk chocolate	2 oz. milk chocolate
2 teaspoons water	2 teaspoons water	2 teaspoons water
angelica	angelica	candied angelica leaves
few crystallised violets	few crystallised violets	few crystallised violets
4 oz. chopped nuts	100 g. chopped nuts	1 cup chopped nuts

Cream the butter and sugar, and add the cocoa and syrup. Mix well and blend in the biscuit crumbs. Press mixture into a greased 6-inch (15-cm.) bottomless cake tin or flan ring placed on a baking sheet. Leave in a cold place for 4 hours before removing the flan ring. Roll in chopped nuts to coat the sides. Melt the chocolate and water in a bowl over hot water and pour over the cake. Decorate with angelica and crystallised violets.

CAKES WITH FRESH FRUIT

Cakes made with fresh fruit and with fruit juices are light, nourishing and appetising, and make a pleasant change from those using dried fruit. When mashing fresh fruit for use in a cake, use a silver fork or spoon to prevent blackening.

Apricot bread

Cooking time: 1¼ hours

Temperature: 350°F., 180°C., Gas Mark 4

Illustrated on page 59

Imperial	Metric	American
1 14-oz. tin apricots	1 400-g. tin apricots	1 14-oz. can apricots
¼ pint water	1½ dl. water	⅔ cup water
2 tablespoons butter	2 tablespoons butter	2 tablespoons butter
8 oz. sugar	225 g. sugar	1 cup sugar
1 teaspoon salt	1 teaspoon salt	1 teaspoon salt
1 egg	1 egg	1 egg
10 oz. plain flour	275 g. plain flour	2½ cups all-purpose flour
1 teaspoon bicarbonate of soda	1 teaspoon bicarbonate of soda	1 teaspoon baking soda
1 teaspoon orange essence	1 teaspoon orange essence	1 teaspoon orange flavoring
4 oz. blanched almonds	100 g. blanched almonds	1 cup blanched almonds

Chop the drained apricots finely. Simmer the water, butter, sugar and salt in a saucepan for 5 minutes. Cool, then add the apricots, well-beaten egg, flour sifted with the soda, orange essence and chopped almonds. Blend well, and turn into a large buttered loaf tin. Bake for 1¼ hours.

Banana bread

Cooking time: 1 hour

Temperature: 325°F., 170°C., Gas Mark 3

Imperial	Metric	American
3 bananas	3 bananas	3 bananas
2 eggs	2 eggs	2 eggs
6 oz. sugar	175 g. sugar	¾ cup sugar
8 oz. plain flour	225 g. plain flour	2 cups all-purpose flour
1 teaspoon salt	1 teaspoon salt	1 teaspoon salt
1 teaspoon bicarbonate of soda	1 teaspoon bicarbonate of soda	1 teaspoon baking soda
2 oz. walnut or almond kernels	50 g. walnut or almond kernels	½ cup walnut or almond kernels

Crush the bananas to a pulp, and gradually work in the beaten eggs, sugar, flour, salt and soda. Stir in the nuts which have been blanched and chopped. Put into a buttered loaf tin and bake for 1 hour.

Blackberry cake

Cooking time: 1½–1¾ hours

Temperature: 350°F., 180°C., Gas Mark 4

Imperial	Metric	American
4 oz. butter	100 g. butter	½ cup butter
4 oz. sugar	100 g. sugar	½ cup sugar
1 egg	1 egg	1 egg
8 oz. plain flour	225 g. plain flour	2 cups all-purpose flour
2 teaspoons baking powder	2 teaspoons baking powder	2 teaspoons baking powder
¼ teaspoon salt	¼ teaspoon salt	¼ teaspoon salt
4 tablespoons milk	4 tablespoons milk	⅓ cup milk

Topping:	**Topping:**	**Topping:**
12 oz. ripe blackberries	350 g. ripe blackberries	2½ cups ripe blackberries
2 oz. butter	50 g. butter	¼ cup butter
4 oz. castor sugar	100 g. castor sugar	½ cup granulated sugar
3 oz. plain flour	75 g. plain flour	¾ cup all-purpose flour
½ teaspoon cinnamon	½ teaspoon cinnamon	½ teaspoon cinnamon

Cream the butter and sugar and beat in the egg. Gradually add the flour sifted with the baking powder and salt, and beat to a smooth batter with the milk. Pour into a greased 7-inch (18-cm.) square tin. Sprinkle thickly with well-washed and dried blackberries. Cream the butter and sugar and work in the flour and cinnamon to a crumble consistency. Sprinkle over the blackberries and bake for 1 hour. Leave in the tin for 5 minutes before turning out with great care.

Orange walnut cake

Cooking time: 45 minutes

Temperature: 350°F., 180°C., Gas Mark 4

Imperial	Metric	American
4 oz. butter	100 g. butter	½ cup butter
10 oz. sugar	275 g. sugar	1¼ cups sugar
2 eggs	2 eggs	2 eggs
8 oz. plain flour	225 g. plain flour	2 cups all-purpose flour
2 teaspoons baking powder	2 teaspoons baking powder	2 teaspoons baking powder
1 teaspoon bicarbonate of soda	1 teaspoon bicarbonate of soda	1 teaspoon baking soda
1 teaspoon salt	1 teaspoon salt	1 teaspoon salt
1 tablespoon grated orange rind	1 tablespoon grated orange rind	1 tablespoon grated orange rind
½ pint orange juice	3 dl. orange juice	1¼ cups orange juice
4 oz. walnuts, chopped	100 g. walnuts, chopped	1 cup chopped walnuts

Syrup:	**Syrup:**	**Syrup:**
8 oz. sugar	225 g. sugar	1 cup sugar
¾ pint water	½ litre water	2 cups water
1 teaspoon grated orange rind	1 teaspoon grated orange rind	1 teaspoon grated orange rind

Cream the butter and sugar, and add the eggs one at a time. Fold in the flour sifted with the baking powder, soda and salt. Blend in the grated orange rind, juice and walnuts, and pour into a 9-inch (23-cm.) square tin. Bake for 45 minutes. Boil the sugar, water and grated orange rind together for 15 minutes, cool and spoon over the cake when it has been cooled on a rack. Cut in squares to serve topped with whipped cream sprinkled with grated orange rind.

Quick orange baba

Cooking time: 20 minutes

Temperature: 400°F., 200°C., Gas Mark 6

Imperial	Metric	American
2 eggs	2 eggs	2 eggs
2 oz. castor sugar	50 g. castor sugar	¼ cup granulated sugar
grated rind of 1 orange	grated rind of 1 orange	grated rind of 1 orange
2 oz. self-raising flour	50 g. self-raising flour	½ cup all-purpose flour sifted with ½ teaspoon baking powder
½ oz. butter, melted	15 g. butter, melted	1 tablespoon melted butter
2 teaspoons warm milk	2 teaspoons warm milk	2 teaspoons warm milk
Syrup:	**Syrup:**	**Syrup:**
1 tablespoon sugar	1 tablespoon sugar	1 tablespoon sugar
juice of 1 orange	juice of 1 orange	juice of 1 orange
1 tablespoon rum	1 tablespoon rum	1 tablespoon rum

Beat the eggs with the sugar and orange rind until the mixture is pale and thick. Fold in the flour, butter and milk and pour into a greased 7-inch (18-cm.) ring tin. Bake for 20 minutes. Turn out and prick at intervals with a fine knitting needle. Make a syrup from the sugar, orange juice and rum, and sprinkle over the cake while still warm. Fill centre with whipped cream.

Orange and almond cake

Cooking time: 35 minutes

Temperature: 350°F., 180°C., Gas Mark 4

Imperial	Metric	American
5 egg yolks	5 egg yolks	5 egg yolks
4 oz. castor sugar	100 g. castor sugar	½ cup granulated sugar
grated rind and juice of 1 orange	grated rind and juice of 1 orange	grated rind and juice of 1 orange
juice of ½ lemon	juice of ½ lemon	juice of ½ lemon
5 oz. ground almonds	125 g. ground almonds	1¼ cups ground almonds
1½ oz. fresh white breadcrumbs	40 g. fresh white breadcrumbs	¾ cup fresh white bread crumbs
3 egg whites	3 egg whites	3 egg whites

Whisk together the egg yolks, sugar, and fruit juices until thick and pale. Mix together the almonds and breadcrumbs, and whisk the egg whites stiffly. Lightly fold in alternate spoonfuls of almond mixture and egg whites, and finally the orange rind. Pour into two buttered and floured 7½-inch (19-cm.) sponge tins and bake for 35 minutes. Cool on a rack and sprinkle with sifted icing sugar, or cover with orange glacé icing (see page 69).

Redcurrant cake

Cooking time: 40 minutes

Temperature: 375°F., 190°C., Gas Mark 5; then 325°F., 170°C., Gas Mark 3

Imperial	Metric	American
2 eggs	2 eggs	2 eggs
5 oz. butter	125 g. butter	⅔ cup butter
8 oz. castor sugar	225 g. castor sugar	1 cup granulated sugar
6 oz. plain flour	175 g. plain flour	1½ cups all-purpose flour
grated rind of 1 lemon	grated rind of 1 lemon	grated rind of 1 lemon
12 oz. redcurrants	350 g. redcurrants	3 cups red currants or tart pitted cherries

Cream the butter and 2 oz. sugar and beat in egg yolks. Fold in the flour and lemon rind, and spread on a greased and floured Swiss roll tin. Bake for 20 minutes. Cool slightly and sprinkle thickly with the clean redcurrants. Whisk the egg whites stiffly and fold in 2 oz. sugar. Whisk again and fold in 3 oz. sugar. Spread the mixture over the redcurrants, and sprinkle with the remaining sugar. Bake until the meringue is dry and hollow sounding when tapped. Cool before cutting in slices and removing from the tin.

Pineapple upside-down cake

Cooking time: 45 minutes.

Temperature: 350°F., 180°C., Gas Mark 4

Imperial	Metric	American
3 oz. butter	75 g. butter	6 tablespoons butter
5 oz. brown sugar	125 g. brown sugar	$\frac{2}{3}$ cup brown sugar
5 fresh or canned pineapple rings	5 fresh or canned pineapple rings	5 fresh or canned pineapple rings
chopped mixed nuts	chopped mixed nuts	chopped mixed nuts
Batter:	**Batter:**	**Batter:**
2 oz. butter	50 g. butter	$\frac{1}{4}$ cup butter
4 oz. castor sugar	100 g. castor sugar	$\frac{1}{2}$ cup granulated sugar
1 egg	1 egg	1 egg
6 oz. plain flour	175 g. plain flour	$1\frac{1}{2}$ cups all-purpose flour
2 teaspoons baking powder	2 teaspoons baking powder	2 teaspoons baking powder
$\frac{1}{2}$ teaspoon salt	$\frac{1}{2}$ teaspoon salt	$\frac{1}{2}$ teaspoon salt
4 tablespoons milk	4 tablespoons milk	$\frac{1}{3}$ cup milk

Melt the butter and stir in the brown sugar until it melts. Pour into an 8-inch (20-cm.) square cake tin, arrange the pineapple rings close together, and sprinkle thickly with nuts. To make the cake batter, cream the butter and sugar and blend in egg; stir in the flour sifted with the baking powder and salt, and then the milk. Pour on to the pineapple and bake for 45 minutes. Turn out and serve fruit side uppermost.

Cumberland courting cake

Cooking time: 30 minutes

Temperature: 400°F., 200°C., Gas Mark 6

Imperial	Metric	American
8 oz. shortcrust pastry	225 g. shortcrust pastry	plain pastry made with 2 cups flour
$\frac{1}{2}$ pint thick sweet apple sauce	3 dl. thick sweet apple sauce	$1\frac{1}{4}$ cups thick sweet applesauce
2 oz. butter	50 g. butter	$\frac{1}{4}$ cup butter
1 oz. sugar	25 g. sugar	2 tablespoons sugar
1 egg	1 egg	1 egg
4 oz. plain flour	100 g. plain flour	1 cup all-purpose flour
Icing:	**Icing:**	**Icing:**
2 oz. butter	50 g. butter	$\frac{1}{4}$ cup butter
2 oz. icing sugar	50 g. icing sugar	$\frac{1}{2}$ cup confectioners' sugar

Line an 8-inch (20-cm.) baking tin with the pastry. Cover with the apple sauce. Cream together the butter and sugar, beat in the egg, then add the flour. Put this mixture on top of the apple sauce and bake for 30 minutes. Leave until cold. Cream the butter and whip in the icing sugar until light and fluffy, and spread on top of the cake.

CAKES MADE WITH PASTRY

Cakes made with pastry are always useful. They can often be made from pastry scraps when meat pies or sausage rolls are on the menu, or can be made from richer pastry in which butter, eggs and sugar are often incorporated, and this type of pastry is particularly good for fruit fillings. When amounts of pastry are specified in the following recipes, the term '8 oz. pastry' means the amount of pastry made from 8 oz. flour.

These pastry cakes can be served with coffee or tea, but are equally good as a dessert or for packed lunches, and provide just the right sweetness to finish a picnic.

Danish cherry tart

Cooking time: 25 minutes

Temperature: 400°F., 200°C., Gas Mark 6

Imperial	Metric	American
6 oz. shortcrust pastry	175 g. shortcrust pastry	plain pastry made with 1½ cups flour
8 oz. stoned cooking cherries	225 g. stoned cooking cherries	2 cups pitted cooking cherries
4 oz. ground almonds	100 g. ground almonds	1 cup ground almonds
6 oz. icing sugar	175 g. icing sugar	1⅓ cups confectioners' sugar
2 eggs	2 eggs	2 eggs

Line an 8-inch (20-cm.) flan tin and prick the pastry well. Fill with the cherries. Mix the ground almonds, sugar and eggs one at a time to a soft paste. Spread over the cherries and bake for 25 minutes. Serve cold.

Honey currant turnovers

Cooking time: 15 minutes

Temperature: 425°F., 220°C., Gas Mark 7

Imperial	Metric	American
8 oz. shortcrust pastry	225 g. shortcrust pastry	plain pastry made with 2 cups flour
6 oz. currants	175 g. currants	1 cup currants
3 oz. sugar	75 g. sugar	6 tablespoons sugar
1 tablespoon honey	1 tablespoon honey	1 tablespoon honey
1 tablespoon lemon juice	1 tablespoon lemon juice	1 tablespoon lemon juice
2 teaspoons melted butter	2 teaspoons melted butter	2 teaspoons melted butter

Roll out pastry and cut into 4-inch (10-cm.) circles or squares. Simmer the currants in a little water until they are tender and plump and the water has completely evaporated. Add the sugar, honey, lemon juice and butter and mix well together. Put a spoonful of filling in the centre of each circle of pastry. Damp the edges and pinch them together. Bake for 15 minutes. Remove from the oven and sprinkle with castor sugar. Serve hot or cold.

Bavarian apple cake

Cooking time: 40 minutes

Temperature: 350°F., 180°C.,
   Gas Mark 4

Imperial	Metric	American
6 oz. plain flour	175 g. plain flour	1½ cups all-purpose flour
4 oz. butter	100 g. butter	½ cup butter
3 tablespoons milk	3 tablespoons milk	¼ cup milk
1½ lb. hard sweet apples	700 g. hard sweet apples	1½ lb. hard sweet apples
2 oz. mixed dried fruit	50 g. mixed dried fruit	⅓ cup mixed dried fruit
2 oz. brown sugar	50 g. brown sugar	¼ cup brown sugar
1½ oz. chopped candied peel	40 g. chopped candied peel	¼ cup chopped candied peel
pinch each nutmeg, ginger, cinnamon	pinch each nutmeg, ginger, cinnamon	pinch each nutmeg, ginger, cinnamon
2 tablespoons fresh white breadcrumbs	2 tablespoons fresh white breadcrumbs	3 tablespoons fresh white bread crumbs

Sift the flour into a basin, rub in the butter until the mixture is like fine breadcrumbs, and mix to a dough with the milk. Roll out thinly to a rectangle and place on a greased baking sheet. Peel and slice the apples and mix with the dried fruit, sugar, peel, spices and crumbs. Put the fruit mixture down the centre of the pastry, leaving about 2 inches (5 cm.) clear at each side. Fold the edges over the fruit, leaving a narrow strip visible down the centre. Bake for 40 minutes, until golden. Cool before cutting into pieces.

Bakewell tart

Cooking time: 40 minutes

Temperature: 350°F., 180°C.,
   Gas Mark 4

Imperial	Metric	American
8 oz. puff pastry	225 g. puff pastry	puff pastry made with 2 cups flour
8 oz. jam	225 g. jam	⅔ cup jam
4 oz. butter	100 g. butter	½ cup butter
4 oz. sugar	100 g. sugar	½ cup sugar
2 eggs	2 eggs	2 eggs
4 oz. ground almonds	100 g. ground almonds	1 cup ground almonds

Line an 8-inch (20-cm.) pie plate with pastry and spread thickly with the jam. Melt the butter, stir in the sugar, then the beaten eggs and almonds. Beat well together and put over the jam. Bake for 40 minutes.

Banbury cakes

Cooking time: 25 minutes

Temperature: 450°F., 230°C.,
   Gas Mark 8

Imperial	Metric	American
8 oz. puff pastry	225 g. puff pastry	puff pastry made with 2 cups flour
2 oz. butter	50 g. butter	¼ cup butter
2 oz. brown sugar	50 g. brown sugar	¼ cup brown sugar
1 egg yolk	1 egg yolk	1 egg yolk
4 oz. currants	100 g. currants	⅔ cup currants
2 oz. chopped candied peel	50 g. chopped candied peel	⅓ cup chopped candied peel
2 tablespoons ground almonds	2 tablespoons ground almonds	3 tablespoons ground almonds
¼ teaspoon mixed spice	¼ teaspoon mixed spice	¼ teaspoon mixed spice

Roll out the pastry thinly and cut into 5-inch (13-cm.) rounds. Cream together the butter and sugar until soft, beat in the egg yolk, then the currants, peel, almonds and spice. Put a teaspoon of this filling on each pastry round, and draw the edges together, moistening the top edge. Press lightly together and form into an oval. Turn over and flatten with the hand. Brush with milk and sprinkle thickly with sugar, and bake for 25 minutes.

SMALL PARTY CAKES

These cakes are all simple to make, but the addition of icing or cream makes them suitable for serving at tea or coffee parties, or even for a fork supper or informal dinner party.

Prune brandy snaps

Cooking time: 7–10 minutes

Temperature: 350°F., 180°C., Gas Mark 4

Imperial	Metric	American
4 oz. butter or margarine	100 g. butter or margarine	½ cup butter or margarine
4 oz. castor sugar	100 g. castor sugar	½ cup granulated sugar
4 tablespoons golden syrup	4 tablespoons golden syrup	⅓ cup corn syrup and molasses mixed
4 oz. plain flour	100 g. plain flour	1 cup all-purpose flour
½ teaspoon ground ginger	½ teaspoon ground ginger	½ teaspoon ground ginger
½ teaspoon grated lemon rind	½ teaspoon grated lemon rind	½ teaspoon grated lemon rind
Filling:	**Filling:**	**Filling:**
8 oz. brandied prunes	225 g. brandied prunes	2 cups brandied prunes
¼ pint double cream	1½ dl. double cream	⅔ cup whipping cream

The brandied prunes should be made a few days in advance. To do this plump the prunes overnight in cold water, then bring to the boil, strain and place in a glass jar. Cover with brandy and leave for several days before using.

Melt the fat, sugar and syrup in a saucepan, remove from the heat and stir in flour, ginger and lemon rind. Drop in teaspoonfuls on a greased baking tray about 2 inches (5 cm.) apart, and bake for 7–10 minutes until just golden brown. Remove from the tray while still warm and roll round greased handles of wooden spoons (to help with the rolling, keep baking tray warm so that the biscuits do not cool too rapidly and become brittle). Slip off when cold and fill with whipped cream mixed with chopped brandied prunes.

Wasps' nests

Cooking time: 25 minutes

Temperature: 300°F., 150°C., Gas Mark 2

Imperial	Metric	American
4 oz. sugar	100 g. sugar	½ cup sugar
4 tablespoons water	4 tablespoons water	⅓ cup water
8 oz. blanched slivered almonds	225 g. blanched slivered almonds	2 cups blanched slivered almonds
3 egg whites	3 egg whites	3 egg whites
8 oz. icing sugar	225 g. icing sugar	1⅔ cups confectioners' sugar
1 oz. plain chocolate, grated	25 g. plain chocolate, grated	¼ cup grated semi-sweet chocolate

Cook the sugar and water to 240°F. or until it spins a thread and stir in the almonds. Beat the egg whites until stiff, beat in the icing sugar, then the grated chocolate and almond mixture. Arrange in very small spoonfuls on buttered and floured baking sheets and bake for 25 minutes. Leave to stand for 10 minutes before removing from the tin.

Coconut kisses

Cooking time: 20 minutes

Temperature: 350°F., 180°C., Gas Mark 4

Imperial	Metric	American
4 egg whites	4 egg whites	4 egg whites
½ teaspoon salt	½ teaspoon salt	½ teaspoon salt
10 oz. castor sugar	275 g. castor sugar	1¼ cups granulated sugar
6 oz. desiccated coconut	175 g. desiccated coconut	2 cups shredded coconut
glacé cherries	glacé cherries	candied cherries

Put the egg whites in a basin with the salt and beat until stiff but not dry. Add the sugar an ounce at a time, beating until dissolved. Lightly fold in the coconut and drop in teaspoonfuls on ungreased brown paper on baking sheets and bake for 20 minutes. Slip the paper on to a wet table or board, leave to stand for 1 minute, then loosen with palette knife and cool on wire racks. Top each with a cherry half.

Meringues

Cooking time: 1 hour

Temperature: 250°F., 130°C., Gas Mark ½

Illustrated on page 51

Imperial	Metric	American
2 egg whites	2 egg whites	2 egg whites
4 oz. castor sugar	100 g. castor sugar	½ cup castor sugar

Beat the egg whites until they stand in stiff peaks but are not dry. Fold in remaining sugar, and shape with a spoon or meringue tube on a baking sheet covered with plain white paper. Bake for 1 hour. Remove the meringues from the paper, and put together in pairs with cream or ice cream.
Variation
Mushroom meringues: Shape the meringue mixture in rounds the size of mushroom caps, sprinkling them with grated chocolate or cocoa shortly before baking. At the same time shape small stems and bake these. Fix the caps to the stems with a little butter icing (see page 70) or thick cream.

Florentines

Cooking time: 10 minutes

Temperature: 375°F., 190°C., Gas Mark 5

Illustrated on page 27

Imperial	Metric	American
3 oz. castor sugar	75 g. castor sugar	6 tablespoons granulated sugar
4 tablespoons cream, or	4 tablespoons cream, or	⅓ cup cream, or ¼ cup
2 oz. butter and	50 g. butter and	butter and 1 tablespoon
1 tablespoon milk	1 tablespoon milk	milk
3 oz. slivered almonds	75 g. slivered almonds	¾ cup slivered almonds
1 oz. glacé cherries, chopped	25 g. glacé cherries, chopped	2 tablespoons chopped candied cherries
2 oz. chopped candied orange peel	50 g. chopped candied orange peel	⅓ cup chopped candied orange peel
plain chocolate	plain chocolate	semi-sweet chocolate

Put the sugar and cream in a saucepan, and cook gently until the sugar has melted. Stir in the other ingredients and blend well. Put in small heaps on a buttered and floured baking sheet and flatten with a knife. Bake for 10 minutes. Remove from the tin and cool, then coat bottoms with plain melted chocolate, marking lines across the chocolate with a fork.

Walnut kisses

Cooking time: 12 minutes

Temperature: 325°F., 170°C., Gas Mark 3

Imperial	Metric	American
1 egg white	1 egg white	1 egg white
4 oz. brown sugar	100 g. brown sugar	½ cup brown sugar
¼ teaspoon salt	¼ teaspoon salt	¼ teaspoon salt
4 oz. walnuts, finely chopped	100 g. walnuts, finely chopped	1 cup finely chopped walnuts

Beat the egg white until stiff, and gradually add the sugar and salt while beating constantly. Fold in the nuts and drop the mixture in small spoonfuls on plain white paper on ungreased baking sheets. Bake for 12 minutes. Cool for 2 minutes before removing.

Eclairs

Cooking time: 30 minutes

Temperature: 425°F., 220°C., Gas Mark 7

Imperial	Metric	American
Choux paste:	**Choux paste:**	**Choux paste:**
¼ pint water	1½ dl. water	⅔ cup water
2 oz. lard	50 g. lard	¼ cup lard
2¼ oz. flour	60 g. flour	½ cup plus 1 tablespoon flour
pinch salt	pinch salt	pinch salt
2 eggs	2 eggs	2 eggs
To finish:	**To finish:**	**To finish:**
whipped cream	whipped cream	whipped cream
chocolate or coffee glacé icing	chocolate or coffee glacé icing	chocolate or coffee glacé icing

Put the water and lard into a pan and bring to the boil. As soon as the mixture boils, quickly put in the flour and salt, draw the pan from the heat and beat until smooth with a wooden spoon. Return to the heat and cook for 3 minutes, beating very thoroughly. Cool slightly, then whisk in the eggs and keep beating until the mixture is soft and firm, but still capable of holding its shape. Pipe the mixture in finger lengths on a greased baking sheet and bake for 30 minutes. Using lard in the recipe ensures that these cakes will bake hollow. When cold, fill with whipped cream, and top with coffee or chocolate glacé icing (see page 69).

Variation

Cream puffs: These are best baked with a cover. Glass ovenware is convenient for this, or a tight cover over a roasting tin. Spoon balls of choux pastry on to the greased tin and bake for 40 minutes to 1 hour depending on size. Finish with whipped cream and a dusting of icing sugar.

Chocolate crispies

Imperial	Metric	American
4 oz. plain chocolate	100 g. plain chocolate	⅔ cup semi-sweet chocolate pieces
½ oz. white cooking fat	15 g. white cooking fat	1 tablespoon white shortening
2 oz. sultanas	50 g. sultanas	⅓ cup white raisins
2½ oz. cornflakes	65 g. cornflakes	2½ cups cornflakes

Put the broken chocolate and fat in a basin over a saucepan of hot, but not boiling, water, stirring until the mixture is smooth. Take the basin from the heat, and stir in the sultanas and cornflakes until they are coated with chocolate. Drop the mixture into 16 paper cases and leave in a cool place until set firm.

REGIONAL AND FESTIVAL CAKES

The regions of the British Isles have always taken especial pride in their traditional country cakes, many of them associated with religious festivals, particularly Easter. Shrewsbury cakes and Tansy cakes, Johnny cakes, Popovers, Pikelets and Singin' hinnies were special Easter cakes, as were the mincemeat and pastry confections variously known as Banbury cakes, Eccles cakes, Cumberland cakes and Hawkshead cakes.

The Simnel cake, so often sold for Easter, was always presented on Mothering Sunday, to be eaten at Easter. The early version of this cake was made with figs which represented 'fruitfulness in offspring', and Fig cakes dedicated to Palm Sunday are still sometimes made.

Shrewsbury cakes

Cooking time: 15 minutes

Temperature: 350°F., 180°C., Gas Mark 4

Imperial	Metric	American
8 oz. plain flour	225 g. plain flour	2 cups all-purpose flour
8 oz. castor sugar	225 g. castor sugar	1 cup granulated sugar
8 oz. butter	225 g. butter	1 cup butter
¼ oz. caraway seeds	10 g. caraway seeds	2 teaspoons caraway seeds
pinch nutmeg	pinch nutmeg	pinch nutmeg
2 eggs	2 eggs	2 eggs
2 tablespoons sherry	2 tablespoons sherry	2½ tablespoons sherry
2 tablespoons rosewater	2 tablespoons rosewater	2½ tablespoons rosewater

Rub together the flour, sugar, butter, caraway seeds and nutmeg. Beat the eggs with the sherry and rosewater and mix with the flour a little at a time, blending carefully. Roll out thinly, cut into shapes and put on greased and floured baking sheets. Prick lightly with a fork and bake for 15 minutes, without colouring. Rosewater gives a very delicate flavour, and may be obtained from any chemist.

Palm Sunday fig cake

Cooking time: 45 minutes

Temperature: 375°F., 190°C., Gas Mark 5

Imperial	Metric	American
6 oz. dried figs	175 g. dried figs	1 cup dried figs
6 oz. plain flour	175 g. plain flour	1½ cups all-purpose flour
½ teaspoon baking powder	½ teaspoon baking powder	½ teaspoon baking powder
pinch salt	pinch salt	pinch salt
2½ oz. castor sugar	65 g. castor sugar	⅓ cup granulated sugar
2½ oz. butter	65 g. butter	⅓ cup butter

Chop the figs roughly and stew in just enough water to cover until tender, then leave to cool. Mix together the flour, baking powder, salt and sugar. Rub in the butter and mix to a batter with the cooled figs and water. Pour into a greased and floured 7-inch (18-cm.) square tin and bake for 45 minutes. If liked, butter icing (see page 70) can be used to cover the top of this cake, but it is very good eaten plain.

Meringues (page 48)

Simnel cake

Cooking time: 2½ hours

Temperature: 325°F., 170°C., Gas Mark 3

Imperial	Metric	American
8 oz. butter	225 g. butter	1 cup butter
8 oz. granulated sugar	225 g. granulated sugar	1 cup granulated sugar
12 oz. plain flour	350 g. plain flour	3 cups all-purpose flour
1 teaspoon cinnamon	1 teaspoon cinnamon	1 teaspoon cinnamon
2 teaspoons baking powder	2 teaspoons baking powder	2 teaspoons baking powder
pinch nutmeg	pinch nutmeg	pinch nutmeg
4 eggs	4 eggs	4 eggs
1½ lb. mixed dried fruit	700 g. mixed dried fruit	4½ cups mixed dried fruit
4 oz. chopped candied peel	100 g. chopped candied peel	⅔ cup chopped candied peel
little milk	little milk	little milk
1 lb. almond paste	450 g. almond paste	2 cups almond paste
2 tablespoons thin jam	2 tablespoons thin jam	2½ tablespoons thin jam

Cream the butter and sugar until light and fluffy. Sift together the flour, cinnamon, baking powder and nutmeg. Slowly beat the eggs into the creamed mixture, blending in a little of the flour mixture at the same time. When well mixed, add the rest of the flour together with the dried fruit and peel. The mixture should be stiff, but may be softened with a little milk if necessary. Roll out the almond paste to two 8-inch (20-cm.) rounds. Put half the cake mixture into an 8-inch (20-cm.) deep round tin which has been buttered and lined with buttered greaseproof paper. Cover with a round of almond paste and top with the rest of the cake mixture. Bake for 2½ hours. Cool in the tin. Remove from the tin and paint the top with jam. Put on the second round of almond paste, brush with egg white, sprinkle with castor sugar and put under a hot grill for a few minutes to give a granulated crystalline surface. Before finishing off, a circle of flattened balls of almond paste can be placed round the edge of the top (traditionally, these represented the Disciples). The cake may be decorated with a ribbon. and toy chickens and eggs.

Twelfth night cake

Cooking time: 2½ hours

Temperature: 325°F., 170°C., Gas Mark 3

Imperial	Metric	American
4 eggs	4 eggs	4 eggs
12 oz. butter	350 g. butter	1½ cups butter
8 oz. castor sugar	225 g. castor sugar	1 cup granulated sugar
1¼ lb. plain flour	600 g. plain flour	5 cups all-purpose flour
2 teaspoons mixed spice	2 teaspoons mixed spice	2 teaspoons mixed spice
1¼ lb. currants	600 g. currants	4 cups currants
8 oz. chopped candied peel	225 g. chopped candied peel	1½ cups chopped candied peel
4 oz. split blanched almonds	100 g. split blanched almonds	1 cup split blanched almonds

Separate the eggs. Beat the butter and sugar to a cream and mix in the well beaten egg whites. Add the beaten egg yolks to the flour and spice, then add to the butter mixture and beat for 15 minutes. Mix in lightly the currants, peel, almonds, brandy and sherry. Pour into a well buttered and lined 10-inch (25-cm.) deep round cake tin, and bake for 2½ hours.

Christmas eve wigs

Cooking time: 20 minutes

Temperature: 425°F., 220°C., Gas Mark 7

Imperial	Metric	American
3 oz. butter	75 g. butter	6 tablespoons butter
8 oz. self-raising flour	225 g. self-raising flour	2 cups all-purpose flour sifted with 2 teaspoons baking powder
1 oz. castor sugar	25 g. castor sugar	2 tablespoons granulated sugar
1 oz. chopped candied peel	25 g. chopped candied peel	3 tablespoons chopped candied peel
2 teaspoons caraway seeds	2 teaspoons caraway seeds	2 teaspoons caraway seeds
1 egg	1 egg	1 egg
little milk	little milk	little milk

Rub the butter into the flour and add the sugar, peel and caraway seeds. Mix to a soft dough with the egg and a little milk. Put into greased patty pans and bake for 20 minutes. Eat with mulled elderberry wine, or dip in ale.

Harvest Betsy cake

Cooking time: 1½ hours

Temperature: 350°F., 180°C., Gas Mark 4

Imperial	Metric	American
8 oz. barley flour	225 g. barley flour	2 cups barley flour
8 oz. plain flour	225 g. plain flour	2 cups all-purpose flour
1½ teaspoons baking powder	1½ teaspoons baking powder	1½ teaspoons baking powder
½ teaspoon salt	½ teaspoon salt	½ teaspoon salt
4 oz. butter	100 g. butter	½ cup butter
4 oz. castor sugar	100 g. castor sugar	½ cup granulated sugar
2 teaspoons golden syrup	2 teaspoons golden syrup	2 teaspoons corn syrup
½ pint milk	3 dl. milk	1¼ cups milk
8 oz. sultanas	225 g. sultanas	1½ cups white raisins

Sift the two kinds of flour together with the baking powder and salt. Cream the butter and sugar, and add the syrup. Add the flour mixture and the milk alternately, then fold in the sultanas. Put into a buttered 7-inch (18-cm.) deep round cake tin and bake for 1½ hours.

Gloucester lardy cake

Cooking time: 45 minutes

Temperature: 400°F., 200°C., Gas Mark 6

Illustrated on page 23

Imperial	Metric	American
1 lb. basic bread dough	450 g. basic bread dough	basic bread dough made with 4 cups flour
4 oz. white vegetable cooking fat	100 g. white vegetable cooking fat	½ cup shortening
4 oz. brown sugar	100 g. brown sugar	½ cup brown sugar
3 oz. sultanas	75 g. sultanas	½ cup white raisins
2 oz. currants	50 g. currants	⅓ cup currants

Prepare the bread dough and allow to rise once (see page 75). Roll out the dough into a rectangle as for puff pastry. Spread one-third of the lard, sugar and fruit over two-thirds of the surface and fold into three. Repeat this twice more and then set aside to rest. Roll the dough mixture out again, roll up like a Swiss roll and cut into two. Place each half cut side down in greased 5-inch (13-cm.) diameter deep round cake tins. Cover with a clean towel and leave in a warm place to prove. Bake for 45 minutes. Turn out of tins immediately when cooked.

PARTY CAKES

Rich party cakes may be served at a tea party, as the second course of a fork supper or even a formal dinner party, and they need not be frightening to make. The effect of these cakes does not come from elaborate decoration and professional icing, but from a cunning blend of flavours, and a lavish use of cream, fruit and chocolate.

Most of the party cakes in this chapter are quick and easy to make. Many of them may be prepared in two stages, with the basic pastry, sponge or meringue being fitted into normal baking times, and the finishing touches added just before serving.

Pineapple gâteau

Cooking time: 40 minutes

Temperature: 375°F., 190°C., Gas Mark 5

Illustrated on page 55

Imperial	Metric	American
3 eggs	3 eggs	3 eggs
4½ oz. castor sugar	125 g. castor sugar	½ cup plus 1 tablespoon granulated sugar
3 oz. plain flour	75 g. plain flour	¾ cup all-purpose flour
1½ oz. glacé pineapple	40 g. glacé pineapple	¼ cup candied pineapple
½ pint double cream	3 dl. double cream	1¼ cups whipping cream
1 large tin pineapple	1 large tin pineapple	1 large can pineapple
rum	rum	rum
1 glacé cherry	1 glacé cherry	1 candied cherry
angelica	angelica	candied angelica leaves
4 oz. toasted flaked almonds	100 g. toasted flaked almonds	1 cup toasted flaked almonds

Whisk the eggs and sugar over hot water until very thick. Remove from the heat and continue whisking for 3 minutes, then fold in the sifted flour with the diced glacé fruit. Put into a 7½-inch (19-cm.) sponge tin and bake for 40 minutes. When the cake is cool, split and sandwich together with two-thirds of the pineapple which has been chopped and sprinkled with rum and one-third of the whipped cream. Coat the sides with more cream and roll in the nuts. Pipe the top of the cake with cream and cover with neat pieces of pineapple and decorate with cream, angelica and pieces of glacé cherry.

Danish strawberry shortcake

Cooking time: 20 minutes

Temperature: 350°F., 180°C., Gas Mark 4

Imperial	Metric	American
8 oz. plain flour	225 g. plain flour	2 cups all-purpose flour
4 oz. butter	100 g. butter	½ cup butter
3 oz. icing sugar	75 g. icing sugar	¾ cup confectioners' sugar
2 egg yolks	2 egg yolks	2 egg yolks
1 lb. fresh or frozen strawberries	450-g. fresh or frozen strawberries	3 cups fresh or frozen strawberries
8 oz. redcurrant jelly	225 g. redcurrant jelly	⅔ cup red currant jelly

Sift the flour on to a board, make a well in the centre and put in the butter, sugar and egg yolks. Work into a smooth paste and leave in a cool place for 30 minutes. Pat out into a large round ¼ inch (½ cm.) thick, prick all over, bake for 20 minutes. When cold, brush the surface with redcurrant jelly, cover with strawberries, brush over with melted redcurrant jelly, and decorate with cream. If using frozen strawberries, put on the cake while frozen and cover with glaze; the cake should then be made about 2 hours before serving.

Pineapple gâteau

Peach baba

Cooking time: 30 minutes

Temperature: 450°F., 230°C.,
Gas Mark 8

Illustrated on page 59

Imperial	Metric	American
4½ oz. plain flour	125 g. plain flour	1 cup plus 2 tablespoons all-purpose flour
pinch salt	pinch salt	pinch salt
½ oz. fresh yeast	15 g. fresh yeast	½ oz. fresh yeast
½ oz. sugar	15 g. sugar	1 tablespoon sugar
6 tablespoons warm milk	6 tablespoons warm milk	½ cup warm milk
1¾ oz. butter	45 g. butter	3½ tablespoons butter
2 eggs	2 eggs	2 eggs
1 large tin peaches	1 large tin peaches	1 large can peaches

Sift the flour and salt into a warm bowl. Cream the yeast and sugar and pour in the milk. Blend well together, then add to the flour, together with the beaten eggs. Beat well with a wooden spoon for 5 minutes, then cover the bowl and leave in a warm place about 45 minutes, until it has doubled in bulk. Cream the butter until soft, and beat into the dough for 5 minutes. Pour into a buttered 8-inch (20-cm.) ring tin, and leave to prove for 10 minutes. Bake for 30 minutes until a deep golden brown. If you have no ring tin, put a cocoa tin in the centre of an 8-inch (20-cm.) deep round tin and hold it firmly in place while pouring in the batter.

Drain the peaches, reserving the syrup. When the cake is cooked, turn out carefully on to a wire rack, and baste thoroughly with the syrup while still hot. Catch the syrup underneath the rack in a soup plate, and continue pouring over the cake until the cake is thoroughly soaked and glistening. Remove to a serving plate, fill centre with peaches and decorate with cream. Rum or any liqueur may be added to the syrup, and any fresh or tinned fruit can be used.

Walnut mocha cake

Cooking time: 45 minutes

Temperature: 350°F., 180°C.,
Gas Mark 4

Imperial	Metric	American
2 eggs	2 eggs	2 eggs
4 oz. butter	100 g. butter	½ cup butter
8 oz. castor sugar	225 g. castor sugar	1 cup granulated sugar
¼ pint milk	1½ dl. milk	⅔ cup milk
6 oz. plain flour	175 g. plain flour	1½ cups all-purpose flour
2 teaspoons baking powder	2 teaspoons baking powder	2 teaspoons baking powder
1 teaspoon vanilla essence	1 teaspoon vanilla essence	1 teaspoon vanilla extract
4 oz. chopped walnuts	100 g. chopped walnuts	1 cup chopped walnuts

To finish:	**To finish:**	**To finish:**
mocha icing	mocha icing	mocha icing
walnut halves	walnut halves	walnut halves

Separate the eggs. Cream the butter and sugar, and beat in the egg yolks and milk. Sift the flour with the baking powder and mix gradually into the creamed mixture. Add the vanilla and walnuts which have been lightly floured. Fold in the stiffly beaten egg whites, pour into a greased 10-inch (25-cm.) deep round cake tin, and bake for 45 minutes. Leave till cold, then cover with mocha icing (see page 69).

Mallow spice cake

Cooking time: 45 minutes

Temperature: 350°F., 180°C.,
Gas Mark 4

Imperial	Metric	American
6 oz. self-raising flour	175 g. self-raising flour	1½ cups all-purpose flour sifted with 1½ teaspoons baking powder
½ teaspoon salt	½ teaspoon salt	½ teaspoon salt
4 teaspoons mixed spice	4 teaspoons mixed spice	4 teaspoons mixed spice
3 oz. soft brown sugar	75 g. soft brown sugar	6 tablespoons soft brown sugar
3 oz. butter	75 g. butter	6 tablespoons butter
2 eggs	2 eggs	2 eggs
3 tablespoons milk	3 tablespoons milk	¼ cup milk
marshmallow frosting	marshmallow frosting	marshmallow frosting

Sift together the flour, salt and spice. Add the sugar and rub in the butter, then mix to a soft dropping consistency with the eggs and milk. Put into an 8-inch (20-cm.) deep round greased cake tin and bake for 45 minutes. Cool, and split into three layers, filling and covering with marshmallow frosting (see page 70).

Golden lemon cake

Cooking time: 25 minutes

Temperature: 350°F., 180°C.,
Gas Mark 4

Imperial	Metric	American
1½ oz. butter	40 g. butter	3 tablespoons butter
6 oz. castor sugar	175 g. castor sugar	¾ cup granulated sugar
3 egg yolks	3 egg yolks	3 egg yolks
¼ teaspoon lemon essence	¼ teaspoon lemon essence	¼ teaspoon lemon flavoring
6 oz. self-raising flour	175 g. self-raising flour	1½ cups all-purpose flour sifted with 1½ teaspoons baking powder
¼ pint milk	1½ dl. milk	⅔ cup milk
pinch salt	pinch salt	pinch salt
luscious lemon icing	luscious lemon icing	luscious lemon icing

Cream the butter and sugar until very light. Slowly add the egg yolks and lemon essence. Add the flour alternately with the milk and beat well with the salt. Grease and line two 8-inch (20-cm.) sandwich tins, pour in the cake mixture and bake for 25 minutes. Cool and fill and cover with luscious lemon icing (see page 70).

Portuguese walnut cake

Cooking time: 45 minutes

Temperature: 350°F., 180°C.,
Gas Mark 4

Imperial	Metric	American
4½ oz. shelled walnuts	125 g. shelled walnuts	generous 1 cup shelled walnuts
4 eggs	4 eggs	4 eggs
4½ oz. castor sugar	125 g. castor sugar	generous 1 cup granulated sugar
coffee butter icing and glacé icing	coffee butter icing and glacé icing	coffee butter icing and glacé icing

Grind the walnuts finely. Separate the eggs. Beat together the egg yolks and sugar for 15 minutes, then fold in the walnuts and stiffly whipped egg whites. Pour into two 8-inch (20-cm.) sponge tins and bake. Put the layers together when cool with coffee butter icing and ice with coffee glacé icing (see page 69).

Gâteau Diane

Cooking time: about 3 hours

Temperature: 225°F., 110°C., Gas Mark ¼

Imperial	Metric	American
4 egg whites	4 egg whites	4 egg whites
8 oz. castor sugar	225 g. castor sugar	1 cup granulated sugar
Filling:	**Filling:**	**Filling:**
4 oz. plain chocolate	100 g. plain chocolate	⅔ cup semi-sweet chocolate pieces
6 oz. butter	175 g. butter	¾ cup butter
2 egg whites	2 egg whites	2 egg whites
4 oz. icing sugar	100 g. icing sugar	1 cup confectioners' sugar
chopped nuts	chopped nuts	chopped nuts
hazelnuts and almonds	hazelnuts and almonds	hazelnuts and almonds

Line three baking sheets with greaseproof paper, mark out 8-inch (20-cm.) circles on the paper and oil thoroughly. Whisk the egg whites until stiff, and gradually fold in the castor sugar. Spread the meringue mixture on the three paper circles, and cook in a very slow oven for about 3 hours until the meringue is dry throughout. Make the filling by melting the chocolate in a bowl over hot water, cooling slightly and adding to the creamed butter. Whisk the egg whites and icing sugar over hot water until stiff and add to the chocolate mixture and mix in thoroughly. Sandwich together the cold meringue layers with the chocolate filling. Spread the chocolate filling round the sides and roll the cake in chopped nuts. Put the remaining filling on top of the cake, cover with chopped nuts, and decorate with hazelnuts and almonds. This cake must be made at least 24 hours in advance.

Chocolate log cake

Cooking time: 6 minutes

Temperature: 450°F., 230°C., Gas Mark 8

Imperial	Metric	American
4 oz. castor sugar	100 g. castor sugar	½ cup granulated sugar
2 eggs	2 eggs	2 eggs
2½ oz. plain flour	65 g. plain flour	⅔ cup all-purpose flour
Icing:	**Icing:**	**Icing:**
7 oz. butter	200 g. butter	¾ cup plus 2 tablespoons butter
5 oz. castor sugar	125 g. castor sugar	⅔ cup granulated sugar
2 egg yolks	2 egg yolks	2 egg yolks
2 tablespoons strong black coffee	2 tablespoons strong black coffee	3 tablespoons strong black coffee
3 oz. plain chocolate, melted	75 g. plain chocolate, melted	½ cup melted semi-sweet chocolate pieces

Pre-heat the oven and warm the sugar in some foil in the oven for exactly 6 minutes. Put the eggs in a bowl and beat in the hot sugar until light, fluffy and white. Fold in the flour and smooth the mixture into a Swiss roll tin lined with greaseproof paper. Bake for 6 minutes. Turn out on a rack, leave till cool and remove the paper. Meanwhile make the icing: cream the butter and sugar until light and fluffy, then beat in the egg yolks, coffee and chocolate until smooth. Spread one-third of the icing on the cool cake, roll up firmly and cover with the remainder of the icing. Mark with a fork to resemble a log and scatter thinly with icing sugar to represent snow.

Peach baba (page 56), and apricot bread (page 41)

CHILDREN'S PARTY CAKES

The big cake for a child's birthday party is usually designed as a showpiece to arouse admiration. The cake design should reflect the age and interests of the child, but as with all decorated cakes the most simple idea is usually the most effective.

A basic Genoese sponge mixture (see page 8) is the best one to use. Glacé icing and butter icing (see pages 69 and 70) will cement pieces together and cover the finished shape. Decorations can include liquorice, marzipan, fruit jellies, peppermint creams, chocolate drops, chocolate vermicelli and coconut. Round chocolate biscuits are easy to use for wheels, and chocolate finger biscuits can help in the making of log cabins and trees.

If you are inventing a shape you want to make, draw a simple diagram on paper and work out first the easiest way to achieve this by using normal cake tins. Round sponge shapes are quickly transformed into animals; loaf shapes may be trimmed into slabs for houses, cars or engines; square cakes make fortresses and houses; and pudding basins give a domed shape for a snowman.

Snowman

Bake a sponge mixture in 1-pint ($\frac{3}{4}$-litre, U.S. $1\frac{1}{4}$-pint) pudding bowl and in two $\frac{1}{4}$-pint ($\frac{1}{4}$-litre, U.S. $\frac{1}{3}$-pint) bowls. Invert the larger cake on board or plate. Sandwich the two smaller cakes together with butter icing and trim to a neat sphere. Fix the head on the body with butter icing, running a cocktail stick through the two pieces for extra security. Ice with butter icing. Make a black paper hat and use a ribbon for a scarf. Use blackcurrant fruit jellies for eyes, nose, mouth and buttons, a liquorice stick for a broom, and a sprinkling of coconut on the cake and board to represent snow.

Easter rabbit

Use one 7-inch (18-cm.) round sponge cake for this. Cut the cake in two semi-circles, and sandwich the halves together upright with butter icing. Stand up on the cut edge. Two-thirds of the way round the cake, cut out a small triangular wedge, and fix this on the opposite bottom edge of the cake to form a tail. Ice generously with butter icing (where the triangle has been cut out will now form the neck of the crouching rabbit). Sprinkle with coconut. Fix pink and white paper ears made from folded white paper with the inside tinted pink. Use chocolate drops or fruit jellies for the eyes and nose. A bed of green-tinted coconut may be sprinkled on the board, and the cake may be surrounded with small Easter eggs.

Elephant cake

Bake two 7-inch (18-cm.) round sponge cakes. Place one in the centre of a cake board as the elephant body. Cut a circle from the centre of the second cake leaving a $1\frac{1}{2}$-inch (4-cm.) border of sponge cake round it. Put this smaller circle beside the larger one to form the head. Cut the remaining ring of cake into four slightly curved 3-inch (8-cm.) lengths, and one longer piece. Place the four shorter pieces at the bottom of the body as legs, and the longer piece as a trunk from the head. Cover completely in butter icing. Use chocolate drops for toenails, cutting them in half. Use a whole chocolate drop for an eye, with a silver ball fixed in the centre. Carve tusks out of peppermint creams.

Owl cake

Bake two 7-inch (18-cm.) round sponge cakes. Place one in the centre of a cake board as the body. Cut a circle from the centre of the second cake, leaving a 1½-inch (4-cm.) border of sponge cake round it. Use this second smaller circle as the head. Cut the remaining ring of cake into two claw feet, a branch to rest them on, and tufted ears. Cover the cake with chocolate butter icing, and make eyes and beak from peppermint creams.

Note: These flat animal cakes lend themselves to almost any shape and are very easy to handle for the amateur cake decorator. Basically, one sponge circle always forms the body, with the second sponge circle forming the head and distinctive features such as tails or paws. A sitting cat, a puppy and a rabbit are all easy shapes. Use chocolate drops and peppermint creams for eyes, mouths and noses. Liquorice strings make good tails. The principle of making these flat cakes can also be used for engines, boats, etc., using square cakes about 1½ inches (4 cm.) thick.

Car cake

Bake an 8-inch (20-cm.) sandwich cake, cut the cake into two semi-circles and sandwich them together with jam or butter icing. Cut out a small wedge from the front of the cake to form the bonnet of the car, and a small wedge from the back to form the boot. Ice the cake with chocolate glacé icing. Make two neat piles of biscuits on the cake board, sticking them together with a little icing. Lift the car body on to them, and stick four chocolate biscuits round to form the wheels. Make marzipan windows, ventilator and mudguards.

Castle cake

Bake a sponge mixture in a rectangular tin. Cut a 1½-inch (4-cm.) strip from the end of the cake and cut this into four equal squares. Cut the remaining cake in half and sandwich together with jam or icing. Fix the squares of cake to each corner to form towers for the castle. Cover the cake with chocolate glacé icing, marking with a knife to represent bricks. Use marzipan for doors and windows, and cut ½-inch (1-cm.) strips into battlements to fix on the tops of the walls. Decorate with toy soldiers and flags.

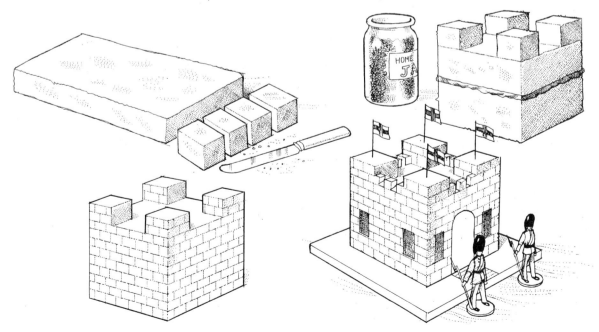

Log cabin cake

Illustrated on page 63

Bake a sponge cake in an 8-inch (20-cm.) deep square cake tin. Cut off a strip 3 inches (7 cm.) wide from the cake. Cut this strip through diagonally from top right-hand edge to bottom left-hand edge. Put these two triangles together to form a large triangular roof and fix to the top of the larger cake to form a house. Make a chimney with marzipan or with a small individual sponge cake, cutting out an upturned V so that it can be easily fixed to the roof. Make windows and a door from marzipan. Coat the cake with vanilla butter icing and fix chocolate finger biscuits over the sides like logs and fruit jellies on the roof. The log cabin may be set in white icing to form a snow scene with snow on the roof and window sills, and small fir trees used as a background. Alternatively, as illustrated on page 63, it can be surrounded by desiccated coconut tinted green to resemble grass with a toasted coconut path.

Train cake

Use a Swiss roll for the body of the engine and a 7-inch (18-cm.) deep square cake to form the cab and trucks. Cut a 3-inch (7-cm.) square of cake and fix it to the back of the Swiss roll as a cab. Cut the remaining cake into oblongs for a coal truck and wagons. Ice the engine, truck and wagons with chocolate glacé icing. Fix a large chocolate biscuit on the front of the engine with a peppermint in the centre. Use marshmallows for the dome and chimney, and peppermints for the windows of the cab. Use peppermint creams for wheels for the engine, truck and wagons. Top the coal truck with chocolates and fill the other wagons with a variety of sweets. Join the trucks together with strips of angelica.

Log cabin cake

BISCUITS AND COOKIES

Home-made biscuits and cookies are treasures. Biscuits and cookies are best stored in a tightly covered jar or tin with paper between the layers. Children particularly love them for tea and snacks.

Basic sugar biscuits

Cooking time: 8 minutes

Temperature: 375°F., 190°C., Gas Mark 5

Imperial	Metric	American
4 oz. butter	100 g. butter	$\frac{1}{2}$ cup butter
8 oz. castor sugar	225 g. castor sugar	1 cup granulated sugar
1 egg or 2 egg yolks	1 egg or 2 egg yolks	1 egg or 2 egg yolks
1 tablespoon cream or milk	1 tablespoon cream or milk	1 tablespoon cream or milk
$\frac{1}{2}$ teaspoon vanilla essence	$\frac{1}{2}$ teaspoon vanilla essence	$\frac{1}{2}$ teaspoon vanilla extract
6 oz. plain flour	175 g. plain flour	$1\frac{1}{2}$ cups all-purpose flour
$\frac{1}{2}$ teaspoon baking powder	$\frac{1}{2}$ teaspoon baking powder	$\frac{1}{2}$ teaspoon baking powder
$\frac{1}{4}$ teaspoon salt	$\frac{1}{4}$ teaspoon salt	$\frac{1}{4}$ teaspoon salt

Leave the butter at room temperature until soft. Work in the sugar, egg, milk and vanilla. Sift together the flour, baking powder and salt, and add to creamed mixture until a firm dough is formed. For rolled biscuits, add about 1 oz. flour to make the mixture stiff enough to roll out to $\frac{1}{4}$ inch ($\frac{1}{2}$ cm.) thickness, chill for 1 hour, then roll out and cut into shapes. For dropped biscuits, drop the basic mixture 1 inch (2 cm.) apart on a buttered baking sheet, and press with a knife or fork dipped in cold water. Bake for 8 minutes. Cool, then sprinkle with sugar or coconut, or cover with glacé icing (see page 69).

Variations
Butterscotch biscuits: Use brown sugar and add 1 oz. chopped nuts.
Chocolate biscuits: Add 1 oz. cocoa and bake at 325°F., 170°C., Gas Mark 3.
Coconut biscuits: Add 2 oz. desiccated coconut.
Date biscuits: Add 2 oz. chopped dates.
Ginger sugar biscuits: Add 1 teaspoon ground ginger.
Lemon biscuits: Add $\frac{1}{2}$ teaspoon lemon essence instead of vanilla essence.
Nut biscuits: Add 2 oz. chopped nuts.
Orange biscuits: Use orange juice instead of milk, and add grated rind of $\frac{1}{2}$ orange.
Spice biscuits: Add $\frac{1}{4}$ teaspoon each of nutmeg and cinnamon.

Tommies

Cooking time: 15 minutes

Temperature: 350°F., 180°C., Gas Mark 4

Imperial	Metric	American
3 oz. ground hazelnuts	75 g. ground hazelnuts	$\frac{3}{4}$ cup ground hazelnuts
4 oz. butter	100 g. butter	$\frac{1}{2}$ cup butter
$2\frac{1}{2}$ oz. castor sugar	65 g. castor sugar	$\frac{1}{3}$ cup granulated sugar
5 oz. plain flour	125 g. plain flour	$1\frac{1}{4}$ cups all-purpose flour
honey	honey	honey
plain chocolate	plain chocolate	semi-sweet chocolate

Mix together the hazelnuts, butter, sugar and flour, and drop in teaspoonfuls on a greased baking sheet. Bake for 15 minutes. Cool and put together in pairs with thick honey. Ice with melted plain chocolate.

Chocolate oat cookies

Cooking time: 10 minutes

Temperature: 350°F., 180°C., Gas Mark 4

MAKES

30

Imperial	Metric	American
4 oz. cooking fat	100 g. cooking fat	½ cup shortening
8 oz. sugar	225 g. sugar	1 cup sugar
1 egg	1 egg	1 egg
2 oz. plain chocolate	50 g. plain chocolate	⅓ cup semi-sweet chocolate pieces
4 oz. plain flour	100 g. plain flour	1 cup all-purpose flour
1 teaspoon baking powder	1 teaspoon baking powder	1 teaspoon baking powder
½ teaspoon salt	½ teaspoon salt	½ teaspoon salt
3 oz. porridge oats	75 g. porridge oats	scant 1 cup rolled oats
1 teaspoon vanilla essence	1 teaspoon vanilla essence	1 teaspoon vanilla extract
1 teaspoon almond essence	1 teaspoon almond essence	1 teaspoon almond extract

Cream the fat and sugar and add the beaten egg. Melt the chocolate and blend in. Sift the flour, baking powder and salt and stir into the creamed mixture. Add the oats and essences and mix thoroughly. Drop by teaspoons on a buttered baking sheet. Flatten with a fork dipped in cold water. Bake for 10 minutes.

Toffee bars

Cooking time: 15 minutes

Temperature: 375°F., 190°C., Gas Mark 5

Imperial	Metric	American
4 oz. butter	100 g. butter	½ cup butter
3 oz. brown sugar	75 g. brown sugar	6 tablespoons brown sugar
1 egg yolk	1 egg yolk	1 egg yolk
2 oz. plain flour	50 g. plain flour	½ cup all-purpose flour
2 oz. porridge oats	50 g. porridge oats	⅔ cup rolled oats
Topping:	**Topping:**	**Topping:**
3 oz. plain chocolate	75 g. plain chocolate	½ cup semi-sweet chocolate pieces
1 tablespoon butter	1 tablespoon butter	1 tablespoon butter
walnut kernels	walnut kernels	walnut kernels

Beat together the butter, sugar and egg yolk until smooth. Add the flour and oats and stir well until smooth. Press the mixture into a 9- by 12-inch (23- by 30-cm.) tin and bake for 15 minutes. Cool slightly. Melt the chocolate and butter over hot water, spread over the warm biscuit in the tin and decorate with walnuts. Cut into bars while warm, but leave to cool completely in the tin before removing.

Almond shortbread

Cooking time: 1 hour

Temperature: 275°F., 140°C., Gas Mark 1

Imperial	Metric	American
7 oz. plain flour	200 g. plain flour	1¾ cups all-purpose flour
1 oz. ground rice	25 g. ground rice	2 tablespoons rice flour
1 oz. blanched almonds	25 g. blanched almonds	¼ cup blanched almonds
3 oz. castor sugar	75 g. castor sugar	6 tablespoons sugar
1 oz. chopped candied peel	25 g. chopped candied peel	3 tablespoons chopped candied peel
6 oz. butter	175 g. butter	¾ cup butter

Sift the flour and ground rice on to a pastry board. Add the chopped almonds, sugar and peel and mix very well together. Have the butter soft and put in the centre of the flour mixture. Gradually knead the dry ingredients into it. Press the mixture into a Swiss roll tin, prick all over, and mark into neat squares. Bake for 1 hour.

Chocolate walnut cookies

Cooking time: 10 minutes

Temperature: 350°F., 180°C., Gas Mark 4

Imperial	Metric	American
6 oz. self-raising flour	175 g. self-raising flour	1½ cups all-purpose flour sifted with 1½ teaspoons baking powder
pinch salt	pinch salt	pinch salt
3 oz. butter	75 g. butter	6 tablespoons butter
3 oz. brown sugar	75 g. brown sugar	6 tablespoons brown sugar
3 oz. granulated sugar	75 g. granulated sugar	6 tablespoons sugar
½ teaspoon vanilla essence	½ teaspoon vanilla essence	½ teaspoon vanilla extract
½ teaspoon water	½ teaspoon water	½ teaspoon water
1 egg	1 egg	1 egg
2 oz. walnuts, chopped	50 g. walnuts, chopped	½ cup chopped walnuts
4 oz. chocolate chips	100 g. chocolate chips	⅔ cup chocolate chips

Sift the flour and salt together. Combine the butter, sugars, vanilla and water, and blend well. Beat in the egg, and stir in the flour and salt. Add the nuts and chocolate chips. Drop by teaspoonfuls on to greased baking sheets. Bake for 10 minutes.

Butterscotch brownies

Cooking time: 20 minutes

Temperature: 350°F., 180°C., Gas Mark 4

Imperial	Metric	American
6 oz. brown sugar	175 g. brown sugar	¾ cup brown sugar
3 oz. butter	75 g. butter	6 tablespoons butter
1 egg	1 egg	1 egg
5 oz. self-raising flour	125 g. self-raising flour	1¼ cups all-purpose flour sifted with 1¼ teaspoons baking powder
½ teaspoon salt	½ teaspoon salt	½ teaspoon salt
½ teaspoon vanilla essence	½ teaspoon vanilla essence	½ teaspoon vanilla extract
2 oz. walnut kernels	50 g. walnut kernels	½ cup walnut kernels

Mix together the sugar and melted butter. Stir in the egg, flour, salt and vanilla essence, and add the roughly chopped walnuts. Spread in a greased Swiss roll tin and bake for 20 minutes. Cool in the tin and cut in 2-inch (5-cm.) squares.

Peanut butter cookies

Cooking time: 10 minutes

Temperature: 350°F., 180°C., Gas Mark 4

Imperial	Metric	American
4 oz. peanut butter	100 g. peanut butter	½ cup peanut butter
4 oz. butter	100 g. butter	½ cup butter
4 oz. castor sugar	100 g. castor sugar	½ cup granulated sugar
3 oz. brown sugar	75 g. brown sugar	6 tablespoons brown sugar
1 egg	1 egg	1 egg
½ teaspoon vanilla essence	½ teaspoon vanilla essence	½ teaspoon vanilla extract
6 oz. plain flour	175 g. plain flour	1½ cups all-purpose flour
½ teaspoon salt	½ teaspoon salt	½ teaspoon salt
½ teaspoon bicarbonate of soda	½ teaspoon bicarbonate of soda	½ teaspoon baking soda

Cream together the peanut butter and butter. Beat in the sugars, egg and vanilla essence. Stir in the flour sifted with the salt and soda, and work into the creamed mixture. Roll small balls of the dough between the palms of the hands, put on lightly greased baking sheets and flatten with a wet fork, making a criss-cross design. Bake for 10 minutes. Cool on a wire rack.

Coconut crisps

Cooking time: 10 minutes

Temperature: 350°F., 180°C., Gas Mark 4

Imperial	Metric	American
4 oz. butter	100 g. butter	$\frac{1}{2}$ cup butter
3 oz. brown sugar	75 g. brown sugar	6 tablespoons brown sugar
4 oz. granulated sugar	100 g. granulated sugar	$\frac{1}{2}$ cup granulated sugar
1 egg	1 egg	1 egg
1 teaspoon vanilla essence	1 teaspoon vanilla essence	1 teaspoon vanilla extract
5 oz. plain flour	125 g. plain flour	$1\frac{1}{4}$ cups all-purpose flour
$\frac{1}{2}$ teaspoon baking powder	$\frac{1}{2}$ teaspoon baking powder	$\frac{1}{2}$ teaspoon baking powder
$\frac{1}{2}$ teaspoon salt	$\frac{1}{2}$ teaspoon salt	$\frac{1}{2}$ teaspoon salt
$\frac{1}{2}$ teaspoon bicarbonate of soda	$\frac{1}{2}$ teaspoon bicarbonate of soda	$\frac{1}{2}$ teaspoon baking soda
4 oz. desiccated coconut	100 g. desiccated coconut	$1\frac{1}{3}$ cups shredded coconut
2 oz. cornflakes	50 g. cornflakes	2 cups cornflakes

Cream the butter and add the sugars, egg and vanilla essence, creaming until light and fluffy. Stir in the flour sifted with the baking powder, salt and bicarbonate of soda. Stir in the coconut and cornflakes, mixing until thoroughly blended. Shape into small balls and put on ungreased baking sheets, rather far apart. Bake for 10 minutes. Cool slightly before removing from the baking sheets.

Spiced coffee drops

Cooking time: 10 minutes

Temperature: 400°F., 200°C., Gas Mark 6

Imperial	Metric	American
8 oz. butter	225 g. butter	1 cup butter
1 lb. brown sugar	450 g. brown sugar	2 cups brown sugar
2 eggs	2 eggs	2 eggs
$\frac{1}{4}$ pint cold strong coffee	$1\frac{1}{2}$ dl. cold strong coffee	$\frac{2}{3}$ cup cold strong coffee
1 lb. plain flour	450 g. plain flour	4 cups all-purpose flour
1 teaspoon bicarbonate of soda	1 teaspoon bicarbonate of soda	1 teaspoon baking soda
1 teaspoon salt	1 teaspoon salt	1 teaspoon salt
1 teaspoon nutmeg	1 teaspoon nutmeg	1 teaspoon nutmeg
1 teaspoon cinnamon	1 teaspoon cinnamon	1 teaspoon cinnamon
1 teaspoon ground cloves	1 teaspoon ground cloves	1 teaspoon ground cloves

Cream together the butter and sugar, beat in the eggs and coffee. Work in the flour sifted with the soda, salt and spices. Put in a cold place for 1 hour, then put in small spoonfuls on a greased baking sheet. Bake for 10 minutes.

Chocolate meringue cookies

Cooking time: 25 minutes

Temperature: 300°F., 150°C., Gas Mark 2

Imperial	Metric	American
2 egg whites	2 egg whites	2 egg whites
pinch salt	pinch salt	pinch salt
pinch cream of tartar	pinch cream of tartar	pinch cream of tartar
6 oz. castor sugar	175 g. castor sugar	$\frac{3}{4}$ cup granulated sugar
6 oz. plain chocolate chips	175 g. plain chocolate chips	1 cup semi-sweet chocolate pieces

Beat the egg whites, salt and cream of tartar until soft peaks form. Add the sugar gradually, beating to stiff peaks. Chop the chocolate roughly, or use chocolate chips, and stir into the mixture. Cover baking sheets with plain paper and drop the mixture on by rounded teaspoons. Bake for 25 minutes, and cool slightly before removing from the paper. Do not fill these meringues with cream.

Giant currant cookies

Cooking time: 15 minutes

Temperature: 375°F., 190°C.,
Gas Mark 5

Illustrated on page 19

Imperial	Metric	American
4 oz. self-raising flour	100 g. self-raising flour	1 cup all-purpose flour sifted with 1 teaspoon baking powder
4 oz. fine semolina	100 g. fine semolina	$\frac{2}{3}$ cup semolina flour
4 oz. butter	100 g. butter	$\frac{1}{2}$ cup butter
4 oz. castor sugar	100 g. castor sugar	$\frac{1}{2}$ cup castor sugar
grated rind of 1 orange	grated rind of 1 orange	grated rind of 1 orange
4 oz. currants	100 g. currants	$\frac{2}{3}$ cup currants
1 egg	1 egg	1 egg
1 tablespoon milk	1 tablespoon milk	1 tablespoon milk

Sift the flour and semolina together and work in the butter until the mixture is like fine crumbs. Add the sugar, orange rind and currants. Stir in the beaten egg and milk to make a stiff light dough. Turn on to a well floured board and knead lightly. Roll out thinly and cut into large rounds with a biscuit cutter. Place on a greased baking sheet and bake until crisp and golden, about 15 minutes.

Chocolate macaroons

Cooking time: 20 minutes

Temperature: 350°F., 180°C.,
Gas Mark 4

Imperial	Metric	American
2 egg whites	2 egg whites	2 egg whites
4 oz. ground almonds	100 g. ground almonds	1 cup ground almonds
4 oz. castor sugar	100 g. castor sugar	$\frac{1}{2}$ cup granulated sugar
3 tablespoons drinking chocolate	3 tablespoons drinking chocolate	$\frac{1}{4}$ cup sweetened cocoa powder
blanched almonds	blanched almonds	blanched almonds
rice paper	rice paper	plain paper

Whip the egg whites until stiff peaks form, then fold in the almonds, sugar and drinking chocolate. Spoon in small heaps on baking sheets lined with rice paper, and put a blanched almond on each. Bake for 20 minutes.

Ginger snaps

Cooking time: 10 minutes

Temperature: 350°F., 180°C.,
Gas Mark 4

Imperial	Metric	American
1 lb. plain flour	450 g. plain flour	4 cups all-purpose flour
8 oz. soft brown sugar	225 g. soft brown sugar	1 cup soft brown sugar
$\frac{1}{4}$ teaspoon salt	$\frac{1}{4}$ teaspoon salt	$\frac{1}{4}$ teaspoon salt
1 teaspoon bicarbonate of soda	1 teaspoon bicarbonate of soda	1 teaspoon baking soda
2 teaspoons ground ginger	2 teaspoons ground ginger	2 teaspoons ground ginger
3 oz. lard	75 g. lard	6 tablespoons lard
2 oz. butter	50 g. butter	$\frac{1}{4}$ cup butter
8 oz. golden syrup	225 g. golden syrup	$\frac{1}{3}$ cup molasses
		$\frac{1}{3}$ cup maple syrup
1 egg	1 egg	1 egg

Mix all the dry ingredients. Warm the fats until they melt, then add the syrup and beaten egg. Beat well into the dry ingredients, and form the dough into a ball. Chill thoroughly, then roll out the mixture thinly on a floured board. Cut into shapes and bake for 10 minutes. Cool on a wire tray.

ICINGS AND FILLINGS

The most attractive home-made cakes are iced very simply. Icing should be spread on a cake with a spoon, palette knife or spatula. When a whole cake is to be iced, tackle the sides first, then put the remaining icing on top and spread. If the sides of the cake are to be coated in nuts or chocolate, spread icing on the surface, then hold the top and bottom of cake and roll like a wheel over the nuts or chocolate spread thickly on greaseproof paper; finish by putting the remaining icing on top and decorating.

For simple decorations, arrange whole or chopped nuts symmetrically on the surface, or use cherries, blanched almonds, angelica or crystallised violets. Chopped nuts, chocolate vermicelli or plain grated chocolate may be scattered on top of a cake. Brazil nuts may also be grated on the large holes to give long thin curls of nut which are very decorative.

A plainly iced cake may also be decorated by dribbles of contrasting icing. A chocolate glaze over white icing is especially good for a chocolate cake. For a feather finish, use glacé icing, making parallel lines of chocolate or pink icing on white, then drawing a skewer across the icing at right angles to mingle the colours.

For roughly finished soft icing, make lines with a fork, or pull up the icing with the back of a wide spoon.

Glacé icing

Imperial	Metric	American
8 oz. icing sugar	225 g. icing sugar	1⅔ cups confectioners' sugar
1½–2 tablespoons water	1½–2 tablespoons water	2–3 tablespoons water

Blend the sugar and water in a basin until smooth. This gives a soft flowing icing but if a firmer consistency is required reduce the amount of water to ¾–1 tablespoon.

Variations

Chocolate glacé icing: Blend 2 oz. melted plain chocolate with the sugar and a little water or sieve 2 teaspoons of cocoa or 1 oz. chocolate powder with sugar. The addition of about ½ oz. melted butter, or a few drops of oil, gives a gloss.

Coffee glacé icing: Mix the sugar with coffee essence or very strong coffee, or blend it with 1 teaspoon of instant coffee.

Orange glacé icing: Blend the sugar with fresh orange juice.

Mocha icing

Imperial	Metric	American
2 oz. butter	50 g. butter	¼ cup butter
8 oz. icing sugar	225 g. icing sugar	1⅔ cups confectioners' sugar
1 oz. cocoa	25 g. cocoa	¼ cup cocoa powder
strong black coffee	strong black coffee	strong black coffee

Cream the butter, sugar and cocoa until light and fluffy. Soften with a little coffee, and spread over the cake, marking with a fork.

Butter icing

Imperial	Metric	American
2 oz. butter	50 g. butter	$\frac{1}{4}$ cup butter
4 oz. icing sugar	100 g. icing sugar	scant cup confectioners' sugar

Cream the butter lightly, then add the sugar and beat until soft and fluffy. Vanilla or almond essence may be added to this icing.
Variation
Chocolate butter icing: Add 1–2 oz. melted and cooled chocolate or 1 dessertspoon sieved cocoa or 1 oz. chocolate powder.

Coffee fudge icing

Imperial	Metric	American
8 oz. icing sugar	225 g. icing sugar	$1\frac{2}{3}$ cups confectioners' sugar
2 oz. butter	50 g. butter	$\frac{1}{4}$ cup butter
2 tablespoons strong black coffee	2 tablespoons strong black coffee	$2\frac{1}{2}$ tablespoons strong black coffee

Heat together the sugar, butter and coffee until the butter melts. Cool for 5 minutes, then beat well and pour over the cake, smoothing with a palette knife.

Marsh-mallow frosting

Imperial	Metric	American
4 oz. marshmallows	100 g. marshmallows	4 oz. marshmallows
2 tablespoons milk	2 tablespoons milk	$2\frac{1}{2}$ tablespoons milk
2 egg whites	2 egg whites	2 egg whites
1 oz. sugar	25 g. sugar	2 tablespoons sugar

Melt the marshmallows slowly in the milk, then leave to cool, stirring occasionally. Beat the egg whites and sugar until stiff and standing in peaks. Fold into the marshmallow mixture, and leave to set a little before using.

Luscious lemon icing

Imperial	Metric	American
1 tablespoon grated orange rind	1 tablespoon grated orange rind	1 tablespoon grated orange rind
3 tablespoons butter	3 tablespoons butter	$\frac{1}{4}$ cup butter
1 lb. icing sugar	450 g. icing sugar	$3\frac{1}{2}$ cups confectioners' sugar
2 tablespoons lemon juice	2 tablespoons lemon juice	$2\frac{1}{2}$ tablespoons lemon juice
1 tablespoon water	1 tablespoon water	1 tablespoon water
pinch salt	pinch salt	pinch salt

Add the rind to the butter and cream well. Cream in half the icing sugar. Mix the lemon juice and water and add to the creamed mixture alternately with the rest of the icing sugar, beating well until smooth. Add the salt and spread upon the cake, marking with a fork.

Chocolate glaze

Cooking time: few minutes

Imperial	Metric	American
2½ oz. plain chocolate	65 g. plain chocolate	scant ½ cup semi-sweet chocolate pieces
2½ oz. icing sugar	65 g. icing sugar	½ cup confectioners' sugar
2 tablespoons castor sugar	2 tablespoons castor sugar	2½ tablespoons granulated sugar
6 tablespoons boiling water	6 tablespoons boiling water	½ cup boiling water

Melt the chocolate over hot water and stir in the icing sugar. Put the castor sugar into the boiling water, and boil together for 5 minutes. Pour the syrup on to the chocolate mixture, beating briskly until the icing is of coating consistency, and pour on the cake while the icing is still hot.

Brown sugar frosting

Cooking time: few minutes

Imperial	Metric	American
4 oz. butter	100 g. butter	½ cup butter
6 oz. brown sugar	175 g. brown sugar	¾ cup brown sugar
4 tablespoons milk	4 tablespoons milk	⅓ cup milk
9 oz. icing sugar	250 g. icing sugar	2 cups confectioners' sugar

Boil and stir the butter and brown sugar for 2 minutes. Add the milk and bring to the boil, stirring constantly. Pour the mixture on to the icing sugar, beating well. Add a little hot water if too thick. This is a particularly good icing for light gingerbreads, spice cakes or individual cup cakes.

Peanut icing

Cooking time: 5 minutes

Imperial	Metric	American
2 oz. butter	50 g. butter	¼ cup butter
2 oz. peanut butter	50 g. peanut butter	¼ cup peanut butter
4 oz. brown sugar	100 g. brown sugar	½ cup brown sugar
4 oz. salted peanuts, chopped	100 g. salted peanuts, chopped	⅔ cup chopped salted peanuts

While the cake is still warm in the pan, spread with a mixture of the butter, peanut butter, brown sugar and peanuts. Put the cake under the grill about 6 inches (15 cm.) from the heat and leave for about 5 minutes until the icing is bubbly and slightly brown. This is good on spice cakes or chocolate cakes.

Ginger ale frosting

Imperial	Metric	American
8 oz. icing sugar	225 g. icing sugar	1⅔ cups confectioners' sugar
½ teaspoon ground ginger dry ginger ale	½ teaspoon ground ginger dry ginger ale	½ teaspoon ground ginger dry ginger ale

Sift the icing sugar and ginger together. Mix to icing consistency with hot ginger ale. Use for light gingerbreads.

White frosting

Imperial	Metric	American
2 oz. butter, melted	50 g. butter, melted	$\frac{1}{4}$ cup melted butter
1 lb. icing sugar	450 g. icing sugar	$3\frac{1}{2}$ cups confectioners' sugar
1 teaspoon vanilla essence	1 teaspoon vanilla essence	1 teaspoon vanilla extract
$\frac{1}{4}$ teaspoon salt	$\frac{1}{4}$ teaspoon salt	$\frac{1}{4}$ teaspoon salt
5 tablespoons cream	5 tablespoons cream	6 tablespoons cream

Cream the butter with a quarter of the sugar, and add the vanilla and salt. Heat the cream, and add to the mixture alternately with the rest of the icing sugar, beating well until smooth. This is one of the few icings which taste good on a light fruit cake.

Rich chocolate icing

Imperial	Metric	American
8 oz. plain chocolate	225 g. plain chocolate	$1\frac{1}{3}$ cups semi-sweet chocolate pieces
4 oz. butter	100 g. butter	$\frac{1}{2}$ cup butter

Melt the butter and chocolate together over hot water. Cool and beat until thick enough to spread.

Simple chocolate icing

Imperial	Metric	American
6 oz. icing sugar	175 g. icing sugar	$1\frac{1}{3}$ cups confectioners' sugar
1 oz. cocoa	25 g. cocoa	$\frac{1}{4}$ cup cocoa powder
2 oz. soft butter	50 g. soft butter	$\frac{1}{4}$ cup soft butter
4 teaspoons hot water	4 teaspoons hot water	4 teaspoons hot water

Sift the icing sugar and cocoa, and gradually blend in butter and water until creamy. Spread on the cake and decorate with a fork.

Coconut frosting

Imperial	Metric	American
6 oz. brown sugar	175 g. brown sugar	$\frac{3}{4}$ cup brown sugar
2 oz. desiccated coconut	50 g. desiccated coconut	$\frac{2}{3}$ cup shredded coconut
2 tablespoons melted butter	2 tablespoons melted butter	$2\frac{1}{2}$ tablespoons melted butter
3 tablespoons cream	3 tablespoons cream	$\frac{1}{4}$ cup cream

Blend together the sugar, coconut, butter and cream and spread on the cooked cake. Leave under a hot grill until delicately browned. This is excellent on Madeira cake.

Butterscotch icing

Imperial	Metric	American
1 egg white	1 egg white	1 egg white
pinch salt	pinch salt	pinch salt
4 oz. brown sugar	100 g. brown sugar	$\frac{1}{2}$ cup brown sugar
2 oz. chopped nuts	50 g. chopped nuts	$\frac{1}{2}$ cup chopped nuts

Beat the egg white until it stands in peaks, then beat in the salt and sugar. Spread the icing on uncooked cake batter and sprinkle with nuts. Follow the usual baking instructions for the cake. This is particularly good for a spice cake or Madeira cake.

Orange icing

Imperial	Metric	American
grated rind of 1 orange	grated rind of 1 orange	grated rind of 1 orange
$\frac{1}{2}$ teaspoon lemon juice	$\frac{1}{2}$ teaspoon lemon juice	$\frac{1}{2}$ teaspoon lemon juice
1 tablespoon orange juice	1 tablespoon orange juice	1 tablespoon orange juice
1 egg yolk	1 egg yolk	1 egg yolk
1 lb. icing sugar	450 g. icing sugar	$3\frac{1}{2}$ cups confectioners' sugar

Add the rind to the fruit juices and leave to stand for 15 minutes. Strain, add the egg yolk, and beat in the icing sugar until smooth.

Seven minute frosting

Cooking time: about 7 minutes

Imperial	Metric	American
1 egg white	1 egg white	1 egg white
6 oz. sugar	175 g. sugar	$\frac{3}{4}$ cup sugar
2 tablespoons cold water	2 tablespoons cold water	$2\frac{1}{2}$ tablespoons cold water
$\frac{1}{4}$ teaspoon cream of tartar	$\frac{1}{4}$ teaspoon cream of tartar	$\frac{1}{4}$ teaspoon cream of tartar
pinch salt	pinch salt	pinch salt

Combine the ingredients in the top of double boiler, and stir until the sugar has dissolved, then put over fast boiling water. Beat with an egg beater until stiff enough to stand in peaks (about 7 minutes). During the cooking, keep the sides of the double boiler clean with a spatula. Flavour to taste.

Honey frosting

Cooking time: several minutes

Imperial	Metric	American
6 oz. honey	175 g. honey	$\frac{1}{2}$ cup honey
1 egg white	1 egg white	1 egg white

Cook the honey to 238°F. (120°C.). Pour slowly on the egg white which has been beaten until stiff. Continue beating until thick enough to hold its shape.

Cream cheese frosting

Imperial	Metric	American
4 tablespoons cream cheese	4 tablespoons cream cheese	$\frac{1}{3}$ cup cream cheese
1 egg white	1 egg white	1 egg white
8 oz. icing sugar	225 g. icing sugar	$1\frac{2}{3}$ cups confectioners' sugar
$\frac{1}{2}$ teaspoon vanilla essence	$\frac{1}{2}$ teaspoon vanilla essence	$\frac{1}{2}$ teaspoon vanilla extract

Work the cheese until soft, then work in the slightly beaten egg white, sugar and vanilla until smooth.

BREAD-MAKING

There is no mystery about bread-making; the rules are simple, the ingredients are cheap and the results are delicious. Here are some basic hints on preparing the best possible bread.

1. Do warm both basin and flour to avoid chilling the dough, which slows up the working of the yeast.

2. Do make the dough rather on the soft side for a light loaf. If the dough is too stiff it cannot expand under the influence of the yeast.

3. Do work the dough thoroughly to ensure an even distribution of yeast through the dough; if this is not done, the yeast will not work properly and the dough will not rise enough.

4. Do keep the dough warm and warm the tins.

5. Don't make the dough too hot or it will produce a very coarse, breakable crumb of irregular texture.

6. Don't try to shorten the rising time of the dough. Under-proving or under-fermentation will give a heavy soggy loaf with a crust that may break away from the top.

7. Don't let the dough rise for too long. Over-proving or over-fermentation results in a loss of strength, colour, scent and flavour.

8. Don't bake the bread at too low a temperature, or it will be pale, moist and flavourless.

Many bread-makers complain that their home-made product goes mouldy quickly. Ideal storage for bread is in a refrigerator, in a plastic bag with the end turned under. The addition of 1 oz. fat rubbed into the flour (for every 3 lb. flour) will help to keep bread fresh longer, or a little malt extract may be used with wholewheat flour.

Any type of cooker can be used for bread-making, and a hot oven is essential. The oven must be preheated before baking. A very large mixing bowl is needed, a wooden spoon, a clean cloth to cover the dough, and loaf tins of the preferred size. Once these tins have been greased and used regularly, they should not be washed but merely wiped clean, and greased and floured for each using.

Ordinary plain flour, both white and wholemeal is perfectly satisfactory for bread-making, and the 3 lb. bag is a convenient size for a batch of bread or buns. In some areas, a 'hard' or 'strong' flour is obtainable, which is preferable to cake flour for bread-making. If regular baking is contemplated, a quantity of flour may be bought direct from a mill, and can be stored for about three months in a small dustbin.

Fresh baker's yeast is cheap and can be kept for about ten days in a covered bowl in a refrigerator, not too near the freezing unit. Dried yeast is very convenient to store and use, though it sometimes has a stronger flavour. The maker's specific instructions must be carefully followed, and only half as much dried as fresh yeast is needed.

Fat and sugar are sometimes added to the basic mixture to give richer, longer-keeping bread. The yeast is often creamed with the sugar to speed up its working time. Salt is an essential in bread and should be dissolved first in a little water, as dry salt affects the growth of the yeast cells.

Before work begins, the flour should be sieved and warmed. Warm water is used, and the approximately correct temperature is obtained by adding one part boiling water to seven parts cold tap water. When the dough is mixed it should be kneaded on a floured board, which means folding it over on itself and pushing with a firm rocking motion until the dough becomes smooth and shiny. It should then be put in a warm basin, covered with a damp tea towel, and left in a warm place to double its size. A rack over a cooker, or in front of a fire, are suitable warm places, but the dough should not be over direct heat or steam.

After this, the dough should be lightly re-kneaded and shaped into loaves, rolls or buns. A slightly stiffer dough is necessary if the bread is to be baked as rolls or freehand shapes without tins. A second proving takes place to be followed by baking in a hot oven.

A container of water in the oven during baking gives a crisp crust. Bread is baked when it sounds hollow if tapped underneath with the knuckles. If it is not quite cooked, it should be returned to the oven without the tins and cooked for a further 5 minutes.

A professional finish gives home-baked bread a more appetising appearance. Plain loaves painted with rich milk or cream before baking have a gleaming brown crust; beaten eggs give a dark crust; melted butter or margarine a crisp, crunchy crust. Thick milk and sugar syrup (1 tablespoon milk to 2 tablespoons sugar) painted on after baking gives loaves and buns a sweet sticky finish.

Bread dough can be kept in a refrigerator after making (kneading, proving and kneading again). Put it into a bowl, brush with melted fat and cover with a cloth. Knead and prove again before using. Yeast dough will also deep freeze, but it will take several hours to thaw before using. It must be kneaded again and proved once before baking.

Wholemeal bread

Cooking time: 45 minutes

Temperature: 450°F., 230°C., Gas Mark 8

Imperial	Metric	American
3 lb. wholemeal flour	1 kg. 400 g. wholemeal flour	12 cups whole-wheat flour
1½ pints warm water	scant 1 litre warm water	3¾ cups warm water
1½ oz. fresh yeast	40 g. fresh yeast	1½ oz. compressed yeast
1 oz. salt	25 g. salt	1 tablespoon salt
1 oz. sugar	25 g. sugar	2 tablespoons sugar

Take half the flour and make into a batter with all the water. Cream the yeast with 2 tablespoons of warm water and mix well into the batter. Cover the basin with a damp cloth and let the batter stand for 15 minutes. Add the rest of the flour, salt and sugar, and make the dough. Mix well and knead for 10 minutes. Warm and lightly grease four small or two large loaf tins, and divide the dough between them. Flatten each piece and roll up to fit lengthwise in the tin, pressing down to avoid cracks and folds. Leave for 1 hour in a warm place until the dough doubles in volume. Bake for 45 minutes, turning the loaves (moving them through a right-angle in the oven) half way through cooking time. Turn the loaves on a wire tray and cool thoroughly before cutting.

White bread

Cooking time: 45 minutes

Temperature: 450°F., 230°C., Gas Mark 8

Imperial	Metric	American
2½ lb. white flour	1 kg. 200 g. white flour	10 cups white flour
2 teaspoons salt	2 teaspoons salt	2 teaspoons salt
1 oz. fresh yeast	25 g. fresh yeast	1 oz. compressed yeast
1½ pints warm water	scant 1 litre warm water	3¾ cups warm water
2 oz. cooking fat	50 g. cooking fat	¼ cup shortening

Put the flour in a large bowl, make a well in the centre, and sprinkle the salt around the edge. Cream the yeast with a little warm water and pour into the well. Add the rest of the water and the warmed fat and mix well to a soft putty-like consistency. Leave to prove until double in size. Knead again and put into two or three tins. Leave to prove again until the bread reaches the top of the tins. Bake for 45 minutes, turning the bread once in the oven. Cool on a wire rack.

Viennese bread

Cooking time: 45 minutes

Temperature: 450°F., 230°C., Gas Mark 8

Imperial	Metric	American
2½ lb. white flour	1 kg. 200 g. white flour	10 cups white flour
2 teaspoons salt	2 teaspoons salt	2 teaspoons salt
1 oz. fresh yeast	25 g. fresh yeast	1 oz. compressed yeast
1 pint warm milk	generous ½ litre warm milk	2½ cups warm milk
4 oz. butter or margarine	100 g. butter or margarine	½ cup butter or margarine

Follow the basic method for White bread. Shape the loaves carefully into long plaits or crescents, and paint them with milk half way through the cooking time.

Currant bread

Cooking time: 45 minutes

Temperature: 375°F., 190°C., Gas Mark 5

Imperial	Metric	American
1½ lb. white flour	700 g. white flour	6 cups white flour
4 oz. sugar	100 g. sugar	½ cup sugar
pinch salt	pinch salt	pinch salt
1 oz. fresh yeast	25 g. fresh yeast	1 oz. compressed yeast
4 oz. warm butter	100 g. warm butter	½ cup warm butter
½ pint warm milk	3 dl. warm milk	1¼ cups warm milk
8 oz. mixed dried fruit	225 g. mixed dried fruit	1½ cups mixed dried fruit
2 oz. chopped candied peel	50 g. chopped candied peel	⅓ cup chopped candied peel

Mix the flour, sugar and salt, and add the yeast creamed with a little sugar. Work in the warm butter and milk, knead and leave to prove for 1½ hours. Knead in the fruit and peel, and shape into loaves or buns to prove for 45 minutes. Bake for 45 minutes, turning after 20 minutes. Small buns will need about 20 minutes cooking time. Remove to a wire tray and glaze with a mixture of water and sugar.

Malt bread

Cooking time: 45 minutes

Temperature: 425°F., 220°C.,
    Gas Mark 7

Imperial	Metric	American
1½ lb. white flour (or white and wholemeal mixed)	700 g. white flour (or white and wholemeal mixed)	6 cups white flour (or white and whole-wheat mixed)
1 oz. fresh yeast	25 g. fresh yeast	1 oz. compressed yeast
¼ teaspoon salt	¼ teaspoon salt	¼ teaspoon salt
¾ pint warm water	scant ½ litre warm water	2 cups warm water
2 tablespoons black treacle	2 tablespoons black treacle	3 tablespoons molasses
2 tablespoons malt extract	2 tablespoons malt extract	3 tablespoons malt extract
2 oz. butter	50 g. butter	¼ cup butter
2 oz. sultanas	50 g. sultanas	⅓ cup white raisins

Sieve the flour into a bowl. Cream the yeast with a little water, and dissolve the salt in the remaining water. Add the yeast and water to the flour, then add the treacle, malt, butter and sultanas. Knead to an even texture, prove until double in size. Knead again and put into tins. Prove until the mixture reaches the top of the tins, then bake for 45 minutes, turning the loaves halfway through the cooking time. Remove to a wire tray and glaze with a water and sugar syrup.

Croissants

Cooking time: 10–15 minutes

Temperature: 425°F., 220°C.,
    Gas Mark 7

Imperial	Metric	American
1 oz. fresh yeast	25 g. fresh yeast	1 oz. compressed yeast
1 oz. butter or margarine	25 g. butter or margarine	2 tablespoons butter or margarine
2 teaspoons salt	2 teaspoons salt	2 teaspoons salt
1½ tablespoons sugar	1½ tablespoons sugar	2 tablespoons sugar
¼ pint warm milk	1½ dl. warm milk	⅔ cup warm milk
12 oz. flour	350 g. flour	3 cups flour
4 oz. butter or margarine	100 g. butter or margarine	½ cup butter or margarine
1 egg yolk	1 egg yolk	1 egg yolk
little milk	little milk	little milk

Dissolve the yeast in a little warm water. Put the 1 oz. fat into a bowl with the salt and sugar and pour over the milk to melt the fat. Leave to cool to lukewarm, then add the dissolved yeast, and gradually add the flour to give a soft, smooth dough. Cover the bowl with a damp cloth and leave for 2 hours. Knead the dough and put into a cold place to chill thoroughly, then roll it out on a floured board into a rectangle. Form the butter or margarine into a square and spread it evenly over the dough. Fold over the dough and roll out to a rectangle, then fold and roll again. Chill once more then roll and fold twice more at intervals of 30 minutes. Roll the dough out to ¼-inch (½-cm.) thickness, and cut into 4-inch (10-cm.) squares. Divide each square into 2 triangles, and roll up each triangle, starting at the longest base and rolling towards the point. Form into crescents and put on a lightly floured baking sheet. Beat the egg yolk with the milk and brush over the croissants. Bake for 10 to 15 minutes.

Brioche

Cooking time: 15 minutes

Temperature: 450°F., 230°C., Gas Mark 8

Imperial	Metric	American
2 oz. flour	50 g. flour	$\frac{1}{2}$ cup flour
1 oz. fresh yeast	25 g. fresh yeast	1 oz. compressed yeast
2 tablespoons warm water	2 tablespoons warm water	2$\frac{1}{2}$ tablespoons warm water
6 oz. flour	175 g. flour	1$\frac{1}{2}$ cups flour
3 eggs	3 eggs	3 eggs
6 oz. butter, melted	175 g. butter, melted	$\frac{3}{4}$ cup melted butter
1 teaspoon salt	1 teaspoon salt	1 teaspoon salt
1 tablespoon sugar	1 tablespoon sugar	1 tablespoon sugar

Put the 2 oz. flour in a bowl and mix with the yeast creamed in the water. Put the little ball of dough into a bowl of warm water where it will expand and form a sponge on top of the water. Put the 6 oz. flour into a bowl and beat in the eggs very thoroughly. Add the butter, salt and sugar and continue beating. Remove the yeast sponge from the water and mix with the batter. Cover with a damp cloth and leave to prove for 2 hours, then knead the dough and leave in a cool place overnight. Half fill castle pudding tins with the dough and prove for 30 minutes. Bake for 15 minutes.

Baps

Cooking time: 20 minutes

Temperature: 450°F., 230°C., Gas Mark 8

Illustrated on page 23

Imperial	Metric	American
1 lb. white flour	450 g. white flour	4 cups white flour
2 oz. white vegetable cooking fat	50 g. white vegetable cooking fat	$\frac{1}{4}$ cup shortening
1 teaspoon sugar	1 teaspoon sugar	1 teaspoon sugar
1 oz. fresh yeast	25 g. fresh yeast	1 oz. compressed yeast
$\frac{1}{2}$ pint warm milk or water	3 dl. warm milk or water	1$\frac{1}{4}$ cups warm milk or water
2 teaspoons salt	2 teaspoons salt	2 teaspoons salt

Sieve the flour and rub in the vegetable fat and sugar. Cream the yeast in half the liquid and dissolve the salt in the rest. Mix into the flour, knead and prove until double in size. Divide into pieces and make into small ovals about 4 inches (10 cm.) across. Brush with milk, put on to a greased baking sheet, prove again, and bake for 20 minutes.

Muffins

Cooking time: 15 minutes

Temperature: 450°F., 230°C., Gas Mark 8

Imperial	Metric	American
1 egg	1 egg	1 egg
$\frac{1}{2}$ pint milk	3 dl. milk	1$\frac{1}{4}$ cups milk
1 oz. butter or margarine	25 g. butter or margarine	2 tablespoons butter or margarine
1 lb. flour	450 g. flour	4 cups flour
1 teaspoon salt	1 teaspoon salt	1 teaspoon salt
$\frac{1}{2}$ oz. fresh yeast	15 g. fresh yeast	$\frac{1}{2}$ oz. compressed yeast

Beat together the egg, milk and warm butter. Put the flour and salt into a bowl, and pour in the yeast creamed with a little warm water. Add the butter, milk and egg mixture, and knead thoroughly to a soft but not sticky dough. Cover and prove for 1$\frac{1}{2}$ hours. Roll out dough to $\frac{1}{2}$-inch (1-cm.) thickness on a floured board, and cut out muffins with a large tumbler. Bake on a griddle, turning as soon as the bottoms are browned, or on a baking sheet in a hot oven for 15 minutes, turning halfway through cooking.

INDEX